Cool School

Where Children Love to Learn

Jane Loosmore

iUniverse, Inc.
Bloomington

Cool School
Where Children Love to Learn

iUniverse books may be ordered through booksellers or by contacting:

iUniverse
1663 Liberty Drive
Bloomington, IN 47403
www.iuniverse.com
1-800-Authors (1-800-288-4677)

Illustrated by Eleanor R. Best

ISBN: 978-1-4697-6597-6 (sc)
ISBN: 978-1-4697-6598-3 (hc)
ISBN: 978-1-4697-6599-0 (e)

Library of Congress Control Number: 2012902216

Printed in the United States of America

iUniverse rev. date: 3/13/2012

In loving memory of Robert Loosmore, MA, teacher and principal of Sir Alexander Mackenzie School (grades one through twelve)
for over twenty years
in British Columbia, Canada

Mr. Loosmore was our ever-present inspiration to do our best.

Contents

Introduction

STARTING SCHOOL AT THE age of six in an all-grades, four-room public school in a small Mennonite village in Saskatchewan, I quickly became used to the idea of cooperative education. Though I came from a large, poor family, I was shy, except when fellow classmates needed help with their schoolwork. Classes usually included about twenty-eight students and three grades, so naturally, not every child received the needed help from the popular teacher; I often helped.

Fast-forward thirteen years. At age nineteen, I became a qualified teacher and taught in small, one-room, all-grades schools in Saskatchewan for five years. By age twenty-six, I had a bachelor's degree in history and had moved to British Columbia, where I taught junior high in city schools for the next five years. Along with my husband (who had an MA in history and a new teaching certificate), I then moved to Bella Coola, BC, where he was teacher and principal of a four-teacher high school that included grades seven and eight. This was a new experience for both of us.

This high school had a history of having no graduates up to that time. Because there were no records of students' progress available to us, and I was the one with the teaching experience, I devised a quick method to sort students by age, grade, and levels of reading, writing, and arithmetic. I also devised a one-page exam for those students around grades eight and nine that tested spelling, punctuation, math, and handwriting. All children were very cooperative with and friendly about the project. By the second school day, we were ready to do some real school work.

Although the students were said to be educationally deficient, they started learning with some determination when their individual needs and interests were being recognized. Some later became active leaders in their community. Other graduates, who went on to attend university in Vancouver, came back pleased to tell us that students from larger communities had appreciated their help writing essays. This experience showed me that excellent results are possible in smaller classes.

Today, working and living conditions both at home and at school have become counterproductive to good child development. With Mom and Dad both working to support the family, parents are not at home as much to give their children the love and guidance they need for personal development. The best parenting books are useful if parents are not too tired to follow their advice. But first, we must improve conditions at school for better child development. Children are finding school boring—with too much daily waiting—and, at times, even unsafe. After they get into high school, they think about dropping out. Our present "modern" system is steadily becoming more dysfunctional. Before it's too late, we must improve the system, ensuring that it becomes one in which every child feels safe, welcome, interested, and eager to learn. It is high time that we try something that is more in keeping with the real needs and interests of our children. This book proposes a viable solution.

Chapter 1

Assessing the Need for Change

IN THE LAST THIRTY (or more) years, a huge change in the way we raise and educate our children has taken place. New technology has changed our places of work, our schools, and our homes. It has changed what we eat, what we wear, how we communicate, how we travel, and even where we live. While taking on these new ways of living, we have unconsciously replaced some of our more effective ways of raising children. Adults have developed an exaggerated faith in the new technology as an answer to the inconveniences of parenting. But rearing and educating children are human problems. Machines are, of course, extremely useful in their right places. However, no matter how good they are, they cannot take the place of an effective teacher or parent.

We haven't taken the time to notice fully the negative impact our busy, comfortable lifestyles are having on child development. We are only beginning to realize that our car and air travel are contributing to global warming; that our very convenient food contains many dubious chemicals; and that TVs, computer games, and the Internet are connected to the waste of our children's precious learning time and to their poor health. So now we are often faced with ever more serious problems related to child development.

One obvious reason it is more difficult to raise children as well as we wish these days is that parents' former support systems are gone. Communities used to be stable and well established. Three generations ago, extended families, relatives, neighbors, churches, and schools were our support systems, as were our traditions, the continuity and consistency of our way of life, and a more natural physical environment. Children experienced little confusion as to what were the wrong and right ways to act and think. Families were large, and technology was primitive. So children were forced to face natural and logical consequences. If you forgot to do your daily job of bringing in the wood and coal for the heater in the house, for example, everybody began to feel cold, and you just knew what to do.

Three generations ago, young people learned about life from other family members. They learned

- how to find raw materials for food and clothing;
- how to work these materials into meals and clothes;
- how to obtain materials to build a complete home; and
- how to enjoy each other through stories told; songs sung; instruments played; plays acted; pictures drawn, painted, or carved; and games played with homemade equipment.

Children learned all these practical and enjoyable skills at home from close relatives and friends. Young and old people were very busy with these activities. Recognition for their efforts and successes was immediate;

schools existed for teaching what children couldn't easily learn at home—mostly reading, writing, and arithmetic, along with some social skills.

Today, for our children, there is a huge wasteland of "free" time every week. Children will tell you that they have nothing to do and how bored they are. Educators have known for a long time that idle children tend to get into more and deeper trouble, which has a way of canceling their better development. We are neglecting to fill our children's time with important and interesting things that they need to actively learn. If our first priority really is children, then we must supply parents and teachers, now and in the future, with the amount of human and material support that is presently missing.

What a Successful Democratic Society Looks Like

The healthiest society is but a step removed from anarchy, a society bound together by the minimum of rules necessary to preserve order and maintain justice. This atmosphere of freedom seems especially to foster and encourage scientific and technological advance.
—Mortimer Smith, in *And Madly Teach the Humanist Library*

Education is a social process ... Education is growth ... Education is not preparation for life; education is life itself.
—John Dewey, quoted in *Time*

The prime purpose of business—in the field of education, this refers to private schools—is to make a profit. Its path to profit is to satisfy some special needs of its customers. A business is privately owned and must function in favor of its owners. A public school, in contrast, is publicly owned and *should be* functioning in the interests of society (though as I highlight throughout this book, this is often no longer the case). Public schools, funded by taxes, are not there to make a profit or to break even. They are there to produce graduates who become competent, effective workers, who have also become interested in and knowledgeable about what is good for their communities, countries, and world. Public schools necessarily have a sense of the importance of community health and strength. The public school's overt purpose is to make possible community life in a democratic country, where citizens of different views and strengths can discuss their common problems and agree on workable solutions. A democratic way of life cannot exist for long without free, quality public schools and universal access to post-secondary education—both of which we are presently losing.

In a successful democracy, we need both public school education and private enterprise. We need a balance of both public and private interests so that they are able to work for the good of all concerned—for the good of people in business and for the good of other citizens like our teenagers, our young adults, and parents who work for a living.

Along with this balance between public and private interests, a democratic society must have community-minded, educated citizens who have the knowledge, attitudes, and skills necessary to be able to discuss, and cooperate with people who have similar, as well as opposing, ideas. Our schools, therefore, should encourage open discussion of opposing views.

A successful democratic society also considers the welfare of all its citizens. Children need a solid understanding of geography and history in order to think about and discuss effectively what should be done for the good of all people. The world is full of serious problems that may lead to the end of all that we believe is good. Too many people ignore the destructive factors—bullying; wars; revenge; new communicable diseases; greed; deep poverty; and pollution of air, water, and soil—in our present civilization. The majority of citizens must be sufficiently aware of their democratic rights and be strong and concerned enough to exercise their democratic muscles. Our next generation of citizens has much to learn about democracy and how it works, if their children are to have anything resembling a happy life. Likewise, schools must set the example for this kind of democratic welfare. All schools, both public and private, should treat all students like equals (with equal rights) even if they are disadvantaged (economically, physically, or socially). Without free public school for all children equally, there can be no effective, educated public. Without an educated, thinking public, there can be no real democracy.

It takes an educated, skeptical, alert public, along with an openly operating, elected government to protect the future happiness and well-being of all citizens. An educated public would be aware of and concerned about the following issues—the environment; the public health system; our parks; support for single parents; legal and reasonable opportunities for the unemployed; hope for a productive future for all teenage children; substantial help for the children of the poor toward security, health, and education; and the problems of discrimination against immigrants and other minority groups in our schools. If we spent more time practicing fairness and generosity, we could save our precious democratic way of life. We need our schools to instill awareness; understanding; and the practice of such virtues as respect, tolerance, and support for each other when one of us is suffering unfairly. A democratic country with an educated public would be well placed to help solve many of the world's problems—especially by example.

In a successful democracy, personal responsibility is essential. With all the distractions in our lives today, many of us are not aware of our civic duty to foster democratic principles as a necessary part of our harmonious way of life. We still elect governments, and more than half the adults still vote at election time. At the same time, however, we have too many people who feel they have next to no say in what the government (that they voted for) does after the election—even when it results in drastic changes in their own living standards.

If our public schools are too busy to teach the importance of citizens taking an active interest in the affairs of their community and in the affairs of their governments, then real democracy will wither and die. As the adage goes, "If you don't use it, you lose it." If citizens are not bothering to exercise their democratic rights and duties, then democracy is not really functioning anymore. Criticizing the health system or complaining about public education in private does nothing to improve the situation—democracy is exercised only when citizens speak up in public in order to improve our methods of doing things or when they exercise their rights to vote.

Now take a look at education and our young people. After students graduate from high school, they want to get a job so that they can become less dependent on their parents. In addition, they very much want to be respected—be it at work, at home, or among their peers. Age eighteen or nineteen—when entering the world of adults—is a critical time. If in the past twenty years, homes, schools, communities, and governments have done their very best to prepare these young people for the demands on them in the next phase of their lives, then these graduates will welcome their new responsibilities with confidence and pride. But if they are facing a work world that they are unprepared for—where conditions may be steeply unfair, wages low, hours long, and they may be made to feel like failures from the start—they will not be prepared for this nasty change. We also have lucky graduates among us who had a very favorable start in the primary grades and for whom good conditions continued until graduation.

Their parents were also able to send them to university for four years. These more fortunate students slide easily into salaried positions designed to keep ahead of inflation. In a functioning democracy, this minority would be a majority.

In short, democratic societies can continue to exist only if child education is high on the government's list of priorities. In a democratic society, it is necessary for the children to learn to think critically, be responsible, master useful skills, and stay healthy. Since children are unable to protect their rights, it is the responsibility of the citizens to demand free education and excellent learning conditions for all children, beginning soon after birth and lasting to about age twenty. Looking specifically at education, parents today can demand and effect an improvement in our public school system, or this is no longer a democracy.

What Our Society Looks Like and Where the Responsibility Lies

For good development, kids need time in the company of interesting, responsible, caring adults. However, children's regular free time is being spent with other children or with adults who are not to be trusted. We try vainly to solve our own child-rearing problems by buying more technology and more expensive clothes and toys. We offer children rewards. We send them to a different school. These techniques do not work for long because we are not removing the real causes of the problem.

Unprotected, unsupervised free time—in most cases (not all)—leads to children having "fun" at the expense and unhappiness of other children. This is harmful to children on both ends of this type of interaction. Because children are bored, they bully (or are bullied), have negative attitudes to most work, wish for new "toys," and spend time looking for some excitement; all of these activities end up costing time and having negative results. Additionally, students are increasingly arriving to class with lazy habits and lackadaisical attitudes, meaning teachers have to work longer and harder to gain their attention and interest. Such a discouraging atmosphere is an unnecessary waste of time to all students in the class, and teachers and parents lose precious time when they have to meet to discuss problems arising from free, unsupervised time for children.

Lack of proper child development and the problems associated therewith are not new. It's just that these problems are magnified and multiplied with the help of technology. The new technology's very attractiveness diverts adult attention away from the modern, unwanted, time-wasting activities children participate in.

Today's five-hour school day is regularly followed by two or more hours of free, unprotected time with bullies, TV, computer games, or a friend, when children think of exciting things to do, like smoking or vandalizing property. Some children innocently communicate with dangerous strangers on the computer. All the above activities help them to forget much of what they learned that morning.

As a society, we are not giving enough money, time, and attention to prepare our youth to eventually step in as intelligent, educated citizens and build a healthy democracy. We certainly need, and could have, twice as many teachers per school as there are now. A teacher with twenty-eight other students in her class will not have time to give a neglected child the extra consideration that such a student must have in order to learn. Sometimes both teacher and parent are expected to do more than is possible. Under present conditions, this is very common. It is not surprising that so many frustrated teachers have decided to go into some other profession.

Consider the problem for the experienced, well-qualified teacher. She has a new class of thirty students, grade five. One child, although rather young, is very advanced and eager to ask good questions. Three are very shy and patient, eight are capable and tend to keep going, but in wrong directions if the teacher is not right there to see what they are doing. Each of the rest of the class has a serious weakness in one or two of the following—reading, spelling, listening, number facts, handwriting, getting down to work promptly, and keeping learning materials in order.

Most of the children are more used to watching TV than to reading a book. They find writing a sentence to be quite burdensome. Many of them have a very short attention span. Respect for authority and for each other leaves much to be desired. Most of them are not used to keeping an organized desk. Their handwriting is not developed enough for what they should be doing, and they are still using "creative" spelling. They will say to you that written work to them is "boring." Believe it or not, all these characteristics are common in today's public schools.

This capable teacher is very limited in what she is allowed to do in order to alter the habits and attitudes of this typical class. Some children ignore parts of assignments whenever they do not feel like (or are afraid of) making the extra effort required. Teachers can't fail these students, for fear the tag of "failure" would crush their self-esteem. However, without some pressure on the pupils to produce, we are stagnating child development.

If we don't manage our children's time better, we will continue to have overworked teachers, overworked parents, overstressed social workers and police, and exhausted friends—all of whom sometimes think of giving up trying so hard because the situation is not improving noticeably. After worrying, working, and spending more time and money than we can afford, similar problems keep showing up. We need a better way—something that really produces the results we had in mind.

Children don't need more toys or more free time; this form of neglect can do much harm to their well-being. What they truly need are better school buildings, more good teachers, and more hands-on learning opportunities. These are the things that keep youngsters interested, safe, active, happy, and in a learning mood.

To achieve better education at acceptable cost, we will need to make our system more efficient. Our current public school system is really very good as far as it goes; it is like a suitable container for collecting grain, but it has a hole through which much grain is regularly lost without being noticed. One of the holes in our mostly very good setup is the regular unnoticed, unsupervised time, when the good work in education is systematically being cancelled. Other holes include excessive class sizes and many technological distractions. As a result, students do not retain lessons that they learned.

Most parents mistakenly believe that, because their own children are doing quite well, they need not worry. I argue to the contrary. A deteriorating society *does* affect the personal growth of all children (including the protected and the well-to-do) in unwanted, indirect ways. For example, the quiet kinds of bullying done in the classroom are effective in destroying the otherwise good learning conditions for those pupils who are aware of the bullying.

In many ways, skimping on education is much too expensive. We are spending more and more on fancy clothes, new cars, and electronic toys, yet we (that is, our governments, under pressure from taxpayers and other interest groups) are trying to spend less on teachers and schools. Without better support from the taxpayers, our children will not be able to develop into productive, dependable, thinking citizens. Instead, many of them will remain unhappy dependents on overburdened, tired parents or on the state (as in institutions like jails, hospitals, shelters, and the like). We all end up paying more for these very unsatisfactory, unnecessary results through increased taxation.

Many parents and other responsible people are not fully aware of the extent of our neglect of the developmental needs of our children. The school day has not increased, but demands on the school have. Public schools have optimistically taken on an extra load of teaching; I'm referring to guidance, sex education, drivers' education, safety, band, community work, fund raising, careers study, and more. These extras mean that schools don't have the time to do a thorough job teaching academic subjects; teachers pay less attention to good sentence structure, vocabulary, research in the library, and neatness in assignments. Yes, schools today are better than those of two generations ago in many ways—mostly as a result of better equipment and better appreciation and understanding among the many cultures that are now represented in our schools. However, teachers today are given less authority and more responsibility. So teachers are trying to do too much for too many children, and too many children do not get the attention they need when they need it. With children, "later" is generally too late. Through their strikes, the teachers in public schools have tried to let us know what is happening to education—poor working conditions for teachers means very poor learning conditions for children.

In our democratic society, we are all partly responsible for what happens. Some people blame the schools for the disappointing behavior and achievement of the children they see. When they blame the schools, they usually blame the teachers. If the teachers are at fault, then so are the parents for letting the children watch videos and TV so much. And so is our "democratic" government for cutting funds from education. And so are all voters who helped put this public school policy in place.

How much is a child's future worth? When we move from small schools to large, consolidated schools served by school buses for ten miles around, we temporarily save some tax money. But the quality of education, in terms of children's safety, health, and social interaction during school, as well as the school subjects they study is much reduced, and children's present and future quality of life deteriorates quite noticeably. This situation is not good for our kids; thus, it is not good for democracy or for the future of our society. We, parents and concerned citizens, must do more than just vote—we need to be involved in the struggle for quality education for all children now, or democracy will soon take a nosedive.

The only humane way we have of reducing and halting the misguided destruction of the future of all people is through more and better public education for all children. Young people, who now need help to learn to become responsible, are an important part of our society. They represent aspects of everybody's future. Therefore, all taxpayers must realize the importance and the advantage, to themselves, of providing the possibility of a balanced, free, quality, public education for all children. All of us— rich and poor—for the sake of our own survival, must recognize the importance of protecting our natural, global environment. It is up to all of us.

For the past ten years, governments have been cutting back funding for public education, which was our biggest hope for the future! Then, to correct the shortage of young professionals in our country, our governments are recruiting trained university graduates from other, poorer countries. All this has helped to develop a long list of very serious problems for our own children's prospects. At the same time, the poorer countries are losing their precious educated young people to the rich countries. Third World countries desperately need their own qualified people to work on their own survival problems. And Canada needs to make employment for Canadian-trained specialists more attractive so they don't get sucked off to the south.

Although the United States and Canada are rich countries, far too many Americans and Canadians are quite worried about the growing unemployment rate, the cutbacks in health and education, and the recent increases in postsecondary tuition fees. With so many education cutbacks and so many problems on the increase for our own poverty-stricken children, it is time we give up on the trickle-down theory and try a trickle-up concept instead.

So often we are told that the young are our greatest resource, and then we fail to support their chances to succeed. What they need is much better teaching and learning conditions to facilitate their success. We should give first priority in the next budgets (federal, state, or provincial) to the health and educational needs of all our young people and their supporting families

When our education system is failing our children, it is not enough that our teachers demand better working conditions so that learning can become more effective or higher salaries to attract and keep our more talented teachers. It has become very important that parents realize that our education system needs their continuing interest and attention and that they demand better public schooling for the young. If we believe that improving our system is entirely up to the government and the experts, improvements can't happen. Why? Because this is a democracy! When enough parents demand a change—such as implementing a new education system like the 2SS, which I'll describe in the next chapter—people will again have much hope for the future.

Always remember that, in a democracy, it is the parents who are the majority. It is really up to the parents to initiate changes in education.

Chapter 2

What Is the 2SS?

I AM PROPOSING *Cool School*, a highly effective, child-friendly kind of public school (grades K through twelve) which, from here on, I will refer to as "the two-school system," or 2SS. The system addresses what I perceive as a need for two schools, rather than one. Essentially, the 2SS is a new kind of public school that selects the best features of the private and the public schools and combines them into one very good, two-pronged public school, which will serve *all* children well. In this book are the broad outlines of what a two-school system would entail.

The purpose of the 2SS is to educate each child to his or her greatest potential for becoming a competent, caring, knowing, reasoning citizen of the world. We need to prepare this young generation for the usual challenges of adulthood and for finding and creating solutions to the problems with the environment and global enmity.

The foci of the 2SS are twofold—competencies and caring.

1. Children will be encouraged to become *competent* when it comes to their
    Health – choosing healthful food and drink and avoiding accidents and communicable diseases
    Safety – avoiding traffic accidents, bullies, Internet predators, and other unsafe situations
    Social abilities – developing consideration for others

Marketing capabilities – mastering skills needed when looking for a job

Fiscal responsibility – maintaining control of one's money

Community participation– gaining skills in getting along well with other people

Academic development – improving levels of literacy, math skills, history, geography, and sciences

2. Children will become *caring* individuals, as staff members and curriculum will foster love, understanding, and appreciation of people of all ages, economic levels, and cultures.

The 2SS will have a policy of caring for each child that will help develop his or her moral character. This will enable students to become parents, who are socially responsible and who live long, happy, healthy, and productive lives, which, in turn, will strengthen the democratic process. In order to achieve these goals, the policies of the 2SS must ensure that all children are encouraged to reach these goals. This chapter discusses the ways that the 2SS would enact these policies.

The 2SS would be, in many ways, very similar to the present public system, incorporating the policies and programs currently in place that are working well. There are really only seven important changes:

1. Smaller schools
2. Smaller classes
3. Schools close to home
4. Longer school days for children
5. More activity courses—especially in the afternoons—requiring modest equipment
6. A free health food cafeteria paid for by the government
7. Content of all courses that is of real interest to each student.

The Commute to School

Through the history of civilization, children have grown up in small communities with the benefit of informal community influence on their development. Parents were less responsible for the child's growth in personality, skills, and knowledge. Community influence has traditionally been very strong. The 2SS is a plan to minimize most of our modern problems in child raising and educating by having our public schools *in smaller communities* or closer to home, where each child's important needs will be easily recognized. As such, the schools would be located within walking distance of children's homes. The many additional benefits to schools that are closer to home include children's personal safety, economy of time and money, convenience, availability of community involvement, and positive effects on the environment. Today's school buses give children a life that regularly includes rushing and waiting—a habitual waste of their precious time and energy.

- Children and parents rush in the morning to get to the bus on time, so that stressed-out parents won't have to drive students to school again. Or if children miss the bus and their parents have already left for work, the children often willingly lose another school day in favor of staying home and watching TV or playing computer games all day.
- After school, there may be another rush to get to the bus stop complete with a loaded backpack and all.
- The school day ends with children waiting in line at the bus stop while worrying about being harassed—even when harassment doesn't happen. On the bus, they wait again, while the bus makes its long journey—as much as an hour or more each way in some cases, even for primary schoolchildren. This repetition is very harmful to any child's physical, emotional, and mental development. More sitting and waiting—more dead time—often means more bullying to suffer or to witness, every school day! Children's time is limited. (Childhood is a short part of one's life.) It must not be wasted and damaged like this.
- On school buses, the use of surveillance cameras instead of responsible supervisors, in effect, means delayed punishment—and *only* for those who are participating in overt wrongdoing that the cameras happen to catch—instead of immediate, positive guidance from a watchful, responsible traveling adult, who can see much more than a camera. The important human touch is missing again.

By eliminating the need for school buses, we also eliminate the woes of idle time and/or rushing.

The School Yard

On the school yard, the 2SS would require two separate school buildings, one for academic learning and another suited to hands-on learning. In the mornings, from 8:00 a.m. to 12:00 p.m. all children would be learning in the academic school. At noon, there would be a free, health foods-only cafeteria for all students and staff. The afternoon school, from 1:00 p.m. to 5:00 p.m., would accommodate mainly the nonacademic activities, such as PE, art, drama, excursions, projects, and the like. The change in activities would keep the learning interesting all day.

These schools should have a flexible limit of about four hundred students—including either grades K through twelve or K through seven—in order to maintain individual contact and recognition of the children's special interests. The two buildings should be on the same school yard but probably far apart. In addition, the two teaching staffs should share an assembly hall with a stage, a library, a storage building, a "sick room" or medical clinic, a health food cafeteria, and a computer classroom.

Children need durable school buildings designed to facilitate learning. New buildings should be designed with the help of experienced teachers, who know best what will encourage our children to become more involved in their projects. Architects would be expected to consult with experienced, successful teachers to design classrooms that are conducive to study, to discussion, and to creative thinking, as well as accommodating the physical aspects of the projects that students would be doing in each of the buildings.

The School Day

In the past three decades, we have added much to the public school curriculum but no extra time in which children can learn. Children must have more school time in order to learn the expanded curriculum. Although freedom is the most precious feature of the political order we call democracy, giving children too much freedom before they have been carefully prepared to handle it constructively, is a serious mistake. Too much freedom too early cancels much of the consistent work done by teachers and parents, who are trying to prepare young people to become cooperative, industrious, well-educated citizens.

To become strong, contributing members in a democracy, children need to learn structure; they cannot afford to waste their precious school days. The idea behind the 2SS is to allow children less "free" time than they get now. Students would be kept interested and occupied most of the school day in small classes or groups under the careful supervision of qualified teachers. In the afternoons, children in this system would have choices of interesting hands-on activities, and in PE, they would be allowed to choose their preferred games. Healthy children would not be allowed to do nothing.

Just think of all the problems we could prevent or minimize by restricting the amount of free time children have—bullying; smoking; vandalizing, overeating unhealthy, convenient foods; experimenting with drugs; stealing; spending excessive time on the phone; watching TV; spending hours on computer games; and teen pregnancies, to name a few.

Not only would the 2SS school day be longer, it would also be carefully structured. How a school uses its time determines whether it is an effective school. If schools—and therefore, students—consider any part of the school day or week (Friday afternoon) or any part of the season (the week before Christmas or the last weeks of the school year) unimportant, then that time is surely being regularly wasted, which is a tragedy for the cause of education. People can waste their youth learning useless skills and information, or their time can be filled with learning necessary skills and knowledge that enable them to function as adults—as desirable friends and citizens. The 2SS replaces harmful and useless learning with pleasant, necessary, and directed or guided learning. Competent teachers lose no time at the beginning of each school period, and they keep the *minds* of their charges engaged to the end of the period. This requires both experience and careful planning. The longer school day would make learning a repertoire of useful knowledge, directions, and skills possible, while preventing students from acquiring harmful habits, attitudes and bad information. The result would be happier people and more cooperative communities.

That said, we must not fail to recognize that some free, undirected learning is also an important part of one's education. For example, a child who has an original idea could be allowed to run with it, while the teacher will see where it leads. If the activity is educational, good; if not, then the teacher will kindly replace it with a more productive topic for the student and for the rest of the class.

A child who is willing and able to present a new idea in class is exhibiting independence—another desirable quality that the 2SS plans to foster.

An On-Site Day Care Center

Locating a day care center near the 2SS could have important advantages.

1. Boys and girls from the school could get some highly interesting firsthand experience in the practice of child care. The nearby day care could be used to acquaint boys and girls with the joys, problems and skills related to raising children at the toddler stages. Sixty years ago, when families were much larger, older children regularly helped in the care and the entertainment of babies and toddlers.

2. It would be convenient for a working parent to leave his or her day care-aged child at the same address as the school the child's older brother or sister attends.

3. Day care as a part of or in proximity to the 2SS would make the eventual transition from day care to primary school smoother and less traumatic for children.

We realize now that children are missing something by not belonging to big families. Both toddlers and responsible schoolchildren would benefit educationally and emotionally from regular, controlled contact with each other.

Food at School

In addition to ensuring structured time, the 2SS would ensure that children's diets while at school were healthful, thanks to government-funded, healthy-foods-only cafeterias.

Current research in nutrition easily identifies healthy foods, and both Canada's Food Guide Rainbow and the USDA Food Pyramid and My Plate make this information readily available.

In schools with over three hundred students, government-funded cafeterias are economical in terms of money, time, health, and opportunities to train and to educate the students. Such cafeterias would yield the following benefits:

1. By not allowing junk food in the cafeteria, nutrition of children could be vastly improved.

2. Children would develop habits

of eating nutritious, healthful food, eliminating the cause of obesity.

3. Very poor children would eat better and, consequently, be able to learn better, and children from well-to-do families would also develop better nutritional habits.

4. Schools would have better opportunities to teach children manners, consideration, and patience.

5. The school cafeteria would be an excellent opportunity for hands-on learning about nutrition, economy, tidiness, and environment.

6. Student appreciation of cafeteria services could be developed by having students take turns helping the cafeteria staff tidy up after lunch.

Class Size

During the past thirty years, people have increasingly gravitated toward the belief that bigger is better. Governments went for large schools because the cost in dollars per head was noticeably less than it was for small schools. Teachers have since been noticing that, in general, children do not develop as well when it is no longer possible to properly monitor the progress and well-being of so many children in a classroom.

Large schools have some important advantages; these include larger libraries and other resource areas; more and larger gymnasiums and playgrounds; multiple auditoriums; larger, more impressive administrative office space; specialist teachers; and noticeable savings to the taxpayer. However, they also have some important disadvantages. Children are bused farther from home, which removes them from their communities and creates wasted time. Big schools tend to have large classes in order to economize on teachers' salaries; this often results in greater use of videos and standardized tests and is not a good learning situation for *any* students (not to mention that large classes turn good teachers into dictators). Larger schools tend to have less parent involvement, and they tend to have more marginalized students. Because they are too busy, teachers often don't notice the quiet bullying that occurs in their presence. Oversized classes are unfair to the teachers, the students, and their parents. At recess, these children are socially excluded from activities or from their own society, or they become the quiet victims of the bullies. Children have little protection on the playground because supervising teachers have too much to watch.

In oversized classes, teachers become poor adult examples to children because the class size necessitates too many regulations, too much paperwork, and too little time to take note of individual students' wants and needs. In addition, teachers have too many worried parents to deal with. It is hard for teachers to help individual students when they can't get to know them well.

The advantages of a small school, on the other hand, include the following:

1. Teaching and learning become very positive experiences.
    a) The very bright students can have the special attention they need to direct their learning, without which they would become bored.
    b) The average students can feel recognized and that the lesson is right for them, and they will suffer no unwanted interruptions.
    c) The students lacking in background knowledge can receive help to correct the deficiency without having to wait.
    d) Students with disabilities can receive consistent accommodation to make learning a pleasant challenge.
    e) Very shy students have a good chance of becoming more outgoing if their needs are recognized.
    f) Very outgoing children will be easier to guide into better learning habits and will become less disturbing.
7. Children in small classes tend to be friendlier with each other and often explain parts of the lesson to each other. This can be a very effective learning situation.
8. In a small class, it is possible to excite children's curiosity so that they *want to know* what the teacher wants them to learn. Thus, they are learning to think about the topic. On the other hand, in a large class, students usually compete for high marks, memorizing for a test to get an A. This kind of learning, although valuable, is shallower and less thoughtful.
9. Teachers are able to give better writing instruction, providing a solid foundation for students' work in other classes. To teach English effectively, a teacher must take the time for lesson

preparation, and he or she must put in many hours of marking students' writings. English teachers of small classes work very hard and often achieve very good results. Therefore, English teachers of large classes must be careful to *not* assign more work than they have the time and energy to mark promptly. We often end up with graduates who do not read or write as well as they need to.

10. It is easier to supervise the playgrounds when there are fewer children, resulting in fewer chances for bullying activities.

11. Principals can do their jobs as leading educators; as they can adequately observe the functioning of their schools, they will be able to make improvements in the right places. Principals can also give subtle recognition to teachers and students who are making an effort toward improvements.

12. Small schools are sometimes organized so that a child has the same (good) teachers for three consecutive years. Under these conditions teachers would be especially interested and involved in the detailed progress of each student—*a huge advantage for the good students as well as for the struggling ones.*

13. Interested, supportive parents will feel more comfortable visiting in a small school.

14. The small school would be closer to home for most pupils, making cooperation between home and school more feasible.

With small classes and competent teachers, children's interests and talents would be easily recognized and exercised. Small schools of three hundred or four hundred students (no more than five hundred) are best suited to offer our children a superior education. The 2SS would have an average of ten and a limit of twelve students per class in grades K through 3. (Classes of more than twelve in K through 3 should have a teacher's aide.) For grades 4 through 12, the average class size would be twenty with a limit of twenty-four students. Additionally, each special-needs student would be counted as three regular students within the class size limit.

Note that class size matters most in the primary grades. This is when the student is most impressionable. Children are different in multiple ways; treating them all in the same way every day—as a teacher must with large classes—does not keep most children interested long enough to want to learn more about the topic. Thus, learning becomes burdensome. With a small class, the teacher is able to touch on each child's special interests while presenting this, now very interesting topic, and then the lesson becomes fascinating. For this reason, primary grades must be limited to about ten or eleven children. It is natural for every child to love to learn. School can become very interesting to a child who was formerly bored. And interest leads to achievement.

Consider the Japanese schools, for example, which are well known for their superior achievement in grade ten mathematics and science as compared with that in the Unites States and in Canada, in spite of their large high school classes. A recent graduate from Japan who studied in our school for one year told me what Japanese public schools were like. In the first five years, classes in the public schools are very small; children feel safe and welcome and are involved in activities that are of great interest to each of them. However, in the higher grades, their classes are rather large and impersonal. Most children do very well, because they come with the strong learning habits they developed in the lower grades. Yet, some still need, or must have the support of a friendlier teacher in order to continue their success.

If primary classes have been small for a child, then he or she will be able to do quite well later on when he or she is in a large class of twenty-four students. But if the students in intermediate and high school have come through the "old" system and have too many learning problems (feeling insecure, poor reading and spelling skill, poor listening skills, and uncertain study habits), then classes will *need* to be kept even smaller—to less than fifteen students, if these unfortunate youngsters are to be given a chance to succeed.

While some students with the proper foundation—as can be achieved in small primary classes—can later do *very* well in large classes of twenty-six to thirty students, this usually happens *at the expense of students who are not so well prepared*. It is better that classes have no more than twenty-four students.

In classes with thirty or more students, those students who need a few minutes of special help early in the school year in order to get off to a good start—perhaps even their first assignment—will typically have to wait one or two weeks to receive that attention; in the meantime, many will give up trying This happened to my ambitious granddaughter, who attended grade twelve in a large city school. After students handed in assignments, it often took a month or two before teachers marked and returned them. There were just too many students per teacher in this school, and classes were too big (on average between thirty and thirty-five students per class) for many willing but neglected learners.

Schools need to be well organized so that thinking children are protected from distractions while they are working through ideas of their own or those taught to them. Creativity requires freedom from interruption. It is an individual activity. To encourage children to think critically and creatively or to do any other kind of original, uninterrupted thinking, we must have space, quiet, and freedom from interference. In the 2SS, classroom time would be free of unnecessary interruptions. This school would have a good library and children who have been taught to like reading. This would be achieved, in large part, with smaller classes and more good teaching.

Class Composition

An effective teacher is one who is both educated and enjoys helping each child learn. This kind of teacher will first make a point of becoming aware of each child's levels of achievement and of his or her strong interests and dislikes. With this awareness, the teacher will progressively become a very effective teacher for each child in this class, including the "weak," the "strong" and the "average."

Years of teaching experience tells us that, for best all-around educational results, separating children into special classes of greater and lesser ability—advanced, average, or struggling—is not as successful for motivating students as is teaching them all together. A broad range of levels within a *small* class has several ways of stimulating the interest and effort of students of each level, providing the class is of manageable size.

Gifted children are properly stimulated and do very well in mixed classes. Students who tutor other students become even more proficient in their subjects of strength, while the weaker students very often understand better from a peer's way of explaining. In this more natural setting, top students are encouraged to excel without becoming too removed from the real world of average achievement. Incorporating the children's different levels of learning into the functioning of the classroom has obvious social benefits, such as helping students develop respect and appreciation for each other. Sixteen years of teaching experience in small classes tells me that gifted children can be stimulated to do very well in mixed, small classes.

Curriculum

The curriculum in the 2SS schools would, at first, be the same as it is now, with a few possible additions, such as hands-on geography and health courses in the afternoon. The 2SS recognizes that children come with different abilities, talents, and interests, so each individual should have some *choices* as to what other subjects he or she studies on top of the core curriculum, which would comprise the three Rs, (Reading, Writing and Arithmetic) for example. The basic curriculum would need to be the same for all public schools. Otherwise, the curriculum will be amorphous, anarchic, and unable to fulfill its purpose for the community. Plainly, the content of the curriculum must be wisely and carefully chosen and the limitations carefully defined so as to include whatever is found to be desirable, while excluding only that which is clearly irrelevant. A public school curriculum must address the needs of our society and, most importantly, the needs of the individual learner.

A teacher who has for a guide a well-established curriculum can set clear and reasonable goals for learning in his or her classes. It will also be possible to provide a highly suitable testing program that will encourage study and give the children fair recognition for work they have done. Regular reporting would also gain the approval and support of parents who would like to know their children's achievement and progress *while* it is happening whenever possible.

The 2SS would have two curricula. One would be for the purpose of improving the child's thinking skills by way of academic courses. The other would be to expand the child's abilities in the practical, the cultural arts, and healthy body building ---- plus the development of good character (kindness, industry, honesty, modesty, determination, forward looking, etc.) would be included in each subject. This would require more equipment and a longer school day. The following sections provide further detail.

Academics

In the beginning, learning the three Rs (reading, writing, and arithmetic) is not as important as learning the right habits and attitudes. A child in the primary grades cannot learn the basics until he or she feels safe, welcome, and physically comfortable. This is made possible by providing good learning conditions, which include a welcoming atmosphere, physical comfort, a small class, effective teachers, consistency in all rules and practices, and safety. Once the child is trained in the ways of the classroom, he or she can begin to progress faster in the academic basics.

Cool School

The basics

In the early years of the twentieth century, our schools taught mainly reading, writing, and arithmetic. Writing was divided into spelling, grammar, punctuation, penmanship, and clarity of the message. Reading was about phonics, pronunciation, enunciation, fluency, vocabulary, and literature. In grades one through three, children learned phonics, oral reading, silent reading, spelling, grammar, vocabulary, English usage (sentences), composition (writing original paragraphs), and literature.

Today, schools spend less than half that time on English because we expect our schools to include a long list of other subjects. The fact that students and parents alike deem English classes as *boring* is evidence that schools have de-emphasized the subject's importance in the curriculum. English has become just one of many subjects. The current public school system does not foster in students the sense of strong accomplishment in this area.

Most people still feel that the central purpose of primary and elementary schools is to teach all children the three Rs to a workable level—a level that is high enough so that the students feel ready to learn the succeeding level in the next grade. This is why we needed schools in the first place. The three Rs are the foundation of academic learning. Schooling without the mastery of the basics is like building a house without a firm foundation. Even with a lot of work, the end result is still pretty shaky.

In particular, there seems to be much talk in the political and educational arenas about the importance of children learning to read, yet we all know of quite a few children who are surprisingly weak in this basic skill. Without being aware of it, the parents, the schools, and the governments in North America are actually doing less and less to include effective reading in the education of our youngsters. Essentially, many people do not properly recognize that competency in English is very important to one's success in learning any other school courses. After graduation, competency in English is again crucial—this is true in one's social life, in one's work, and in one's ability to function as a citizen. But very few parents read regularly to their preschool- and primary school-aged children, usually for very understandable reasons. In my experience, children whose parents do read to them do much better in school.

In schools, the new prescribed readers and textbooks have more pictures and a simpler level of English, with simpler ideas to learn. This has had the effect of excluding from lessons much of the good literature, which is rich in vocabulary, syntax, and interest. In order to know how to use a word, however, a person needs to be able to read, write, and spell it. A few illustrations will help a book reader, but too many pictures will do away with the value of the print—it will weaken the richness of the book's message. This is also true about phrases and sentences. Words, phrases, and sentences embody ideas. We remember ideas and express them in words. Because people can read, they can think much better now than people could before writing was invented. Reading is an exercise that makes the brain bigger, stronger, and more skilled in remembering and thinking.

Strength in reading is, therefore, basic to real education. When we undermine a child's chances of learning to read well, we destroy his or her chances of becoming a happy, competent citizen; we also undermine the very foundation of democracy. In a dictatorship, dictators like to have well-trained, obedient, but otherwise ignorant people, as their subjects. A democracy can exist only as long as the citizens are readers and thinkers about the common good, in addition to being well trained and cooperative in their work.

The 2SS would devote much time and attention toward establishing, in the primary grades, a firm reading foundation in each child, which would lead to a desire in children to read books. An interesting, dynamic library would help. It takes a good librarian to have a functioning school library.

***

Very few children today, however, become avid readers. "Reading is too hard and too boring," says a bright nine-year-old grandchild of mine, as he turns on the TV. Clearly, there is a need to get back to the basics. It's also important to note that children begin school with certain advantages or strengths, as well as with various weaknesses or deficiencies. Some do not understand English. Some fortunate children have had parents read to them for several years. Some have a physical disability. Some are from immigrant families, who know very little about their surroundings, the language, or the customs. Some are just very shy.

The 2SS is set up to ensure that students master basic language skills to a solid level of competency before attempting the next level. Where necessary (as with immigrants or children with some important disadvantage) children will get friendly, competent help individually and in small groups in a daily, scheduled afternoon block, for as long as is necessary to bring each child up to standard level. Once the student is competent in language, all other subjects will become much easier to learn and, therefore, more interesting.

In the 2SS, the goal is threefold. (1) Each and every student must *master* the functions of language (listening, speaking, reading, writing, and numbers). (2) Then, he or she must acquire a solid foundation in the academic subjects (literature, history, geography, the sciences, and math). (3) In the meantime, educators will help each student develop interests and talents of his or her own in the more active, afternoon hands-on sessions. In order to progress to the next grade level in the 2SS, every child in the primary grades must learn to speak, read, and write to a level of competency that enables him or her to feel fully adequate to perform in the next grade. This means that no child gets past grade one until he or she has learned to read, write, and do first-grade math with confidence and is ready to start learning the grade two basics. The same is true for grade two—and grade three. Why? Because the 2SS emphasizes the importance of establishing a strong foundation in the basics *early* in the child's schooling. If it takes special accommodation (such as tutoring in the afternoons for forty-five minutes per day or extra time in the afternoon library period) then that must take precedence over other subjects. Failing language is not an option because language is the foundation for all the learning that follows. With a good foundation, learning becomes a happy experience. Every child has the right to enjoy school. Out of a deep respect for the needs of each child, no student would be allowed to miss learning the basics.

The academic part of the 2SS would also have all children master the basic skills required for studying subjects like history, geography, science, math, and language. These skills include, among others, finding, selecting and organizing information on a given topic.

Remember, the success of the whole school depends heavily on the quality of the primary program. Weakness at the primary level means weakness in the grades following, no matter how good the teachers happen to be.

Second language acquisition

In addition to the basics, second language acquisition is desirous in the 2SS. When one learns a second, (third, or fourth) language, one learns much more than vocabulary and grammar; one also learns another culture, another angle on the world, and new ways of thinking about things. A monoglot is at a noticeable disadvantage. Monolingual tourists miss the significance of many signs and situations that a multilingual person would readily appreciate. A polyglot, even one whose language mastery is poor, connects more easily, even with people who speak another language that he or she has not learned. If it can be arranged, the 2SS would prefer to have children learn a second language starting in the primary grades, from a teacher who speaks that language very well.

Geography

In the 2SS, middle school students will study geography, despite the fact that the subject has been largely crowded out of the school curriculum in Canada and the United States. Before you can understand or appreciate most things (history, a news story, story books, a culture, a language, trade, environmental problems, travel brochures, or your relationship to the problems of other people) you need to *know* geography so that you can relate the new information to what you already know about the map of the world. Geography is a basic—like the number facts in arithmetic—and it lends itself to drawing maps, using pictures, using videos, going on excursions, and preparing student presentations.

In social studies classes, however, we only *touch* on geography. Our children are unable to understand and remember important, new information if they are not able to link this information with a place they already know well. An adult who does not know geography is handicapped when it comes to doing business, understanding people from other places, remembering a story, and much more. It is very unfair to the student not to include geography as a basic subject in grades three to eight.

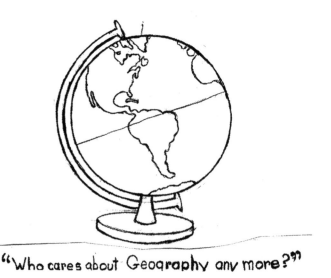

"Who cares about Geography any more?"

Cool School

Politics

The foundation of every state is the education of its youth.
—Diogenes the Cynic

In a democracy, the public school exists for several purposes. An important one is learning several points of view when studying a subject like history, religion, science, and even language. These points of view make the lessons *much* more interesting and easier to remember. This kind of teaching stimulates and exercises the brain, helping students think more deeply, which can become a habit. Thinking sometimes leads to new and better ideas, and that is how our civilization progresses to greater levels.

People educated in this more effective way ask better questions at public meetings and remind politicians to work for the voters. These people are also valuable community workers because they know how to have fruitful discussions. They take an interest in the welfare of their neighbors. They are able to identify their own future well-being with that of the other people in the neighborhood. They are a strength to the community.

The 2SS would promote careful listening, clear explaining, and intelligent discussion. And projects suited to the children's interests would support cooperation. This kind of learning can be achieved when the people involved are given the time and the space necessary to come up with some positive, original ideas. The 2SS includes a plan to develop all children into thinking, questioning, and responsible citizens.

Comparative religion

I've discovered that the same fruits of faith that were in other people's lives were also in mine.
—Sue Tennant

The 2SS, with its greater classroom space and its extended day, could better accommodate voluntary religious education. At no other cost to the community, the different religious groups in the community should be allowed one or two one-hour sessions per week. Having these sessions near the end of the school day would most likely suit the volunteer religious teachers, as well as the regular staff.

This could provide a welcome transition from school to home—a better chance for parents to stay close with their children while they are developing into adults with a positive purpose in life. Beside the spiritual value of religious teaching, there is another advantage; it keeps parents and children in better harmony of attitude.

Beyond Academics

Schools, of today, need to do more than teach children to learn the basics and a vocation. Beyond academic learning, a child has some other very important needs that must be satisfied so that he or she can develop into a functional citizen. Provision for social recreation and for community involvement—involvement that allows children to mix with people both younger and older than themselves—is necessary. Schools must also provide opportunities for learning practical, recreational, social, and artistic skills and for gaining a healthy appreciation for the preservation of our natural environment.

All children should have some choice in what they would like to learn or do. They should be favored with balance in their lives, so that they will become well-rounded citizens. Balance produces more happiness in general. The nonacademic courses offered would depend on community demands and on the availability of equipment and talented instructors. Some examples of useable skills at the child's level may include knitting a scarf, building a doghouse, learning a computer skill, playing guitar, or even preparing a health drink for a social event.

The afternoon part of the 2SS could keep children interested, as they connect academic learning to practical activities. For all schoolchildren, academic education would be reinforced with hands-on projects that match the interests and abilities of each child. The 2SS would have children learn the academic subjects in the morning and reinforce this new knowledge in the afternoons, while engaged in practical, physically active endeavors, such as sports, the arts, visiting the museum, taking science excursions, sketching outdoors, and more. For example, in softball we use numbers to keep score and run outdoors to get exercise to become stronger and healthier.

Depending on the opportunities available and the capabilities of the students the possibilities of the afternoon endeavors can vary greatly. Here are two possibilities.

- Video reports are popular with many young people. Using their language skills, coupled with, perhaps, some musical ability and a great idea they have, students could make a stimulating video.

- Math skills may be integrated with physical activity by observing a salmon run in certain areas of the country. Here salmon are counted and an analysis could be made as a result.

Keep in mind that truly the possibilities are endless!

Consider, for example, how the arts are another form of learning. The 2SS would capitalize on this opportunity to develop young brains by graduating exposure to the arts from the simple to the more interesting. There would be time and space for as many of these disciplines as catch the interest of students. In this system, children would be doing more than watching and listening. Those interested would be developing hands-on skills in the arts of their choices.

Organized physical activity is another important part of the afternoon curriculum. Other than the obvious advantage of better physical health, physical activity also provides students with other important benefits:

1. Regular, socially shared exercise enhances academic learning. The sports program is an opportunity for coaches and other school officials or staff to set an example of good manners and sportsmanship. Good manners as expressed in attitudes and behavior should be *a requirement* of new staff appointments.

2. When coaches, teachers, or referees practice and enforce good manners, consideration for others, and fairness, sport establishes in young people civil behavior, which is conducive to better understanding and friendship between opposing groups.

3. Other than in combat sports (wrestling, boxing, judo, and the like) enforcement of "no-contact" rules is valuable in promoting friendly feelings, avoiding serious injuries, and enabling students to continue participating in the sport long into adulthood. The benefits of enjoyable physical activity could become *much longer* lasting.

4. The competitive team sports one sees on TV are calibrated to occasionally break out into fights and injuries that add to the excitement of paying spectators. When this is part of the sport, some competitors win by "accidentally" injuring an opposing

player. This is *not* sportsmanship! It is not part of a democratic education. It takes some learning to get rid of the nasty side of competition.

The 2SS takes the long-term value of sports seriously. It embraces the needs of all students of all levels of ability. This educational system emphasizes the social enjoyment of being physically active and improving one's health and fitness over the winning of competitions. Friendly competition between *equals* is seen as adding to the enjoyment and continued interest in keeping fit and practicing consideration for others. Competition in sports can be fun for the weakest among us if the competition is about at the same level of ability. This is not hard to arrange in a school.

Between the academic rigors of the morning session and the physical activities (and tutoring) of the afternoon session, students' lunchtime would lend educational opportunities as well. The 2SS would have a special cafeteria that would provide good opportunities for training children to become healthy, environmentally conscious adults. The cafeteria would teach students about maintaining their own health and that of the environment by focusing on important subjects, such as the following:

1. Nutrition
2. Sanitation
3. Respect for people who work for them
4. Manners
5. Consideration for working people
6. Disposal of empty containers
7. Disposal of food not eaten
8. Recycling of paper, plastic, glass, and metal
9. Composting of leftover food
10. Using the well-rotted compost to grow plants (in science class)

The cafeteria could be one place for effective hands-on activities designed to instruct on the above topics. The janitors could eat there and also be in charge of those children whose turn it was to do the sorting and disposal of leftover food and of empty containers and those children whose turn it was to sweep the floor. The people running the cafeteria would be in charge of the children who were doing the serving jobs and those in the clear-the-tables crew. All children would be expected to take their turn and do their share, while the other students would be expected to show their appreciation and respect. All children should take their turns at as many jobs as is convenient.

High school students would need some training in government food standards, training that would teach them the scientific reasons for these regulations. After that, they could be asked to work in the cafeteria for brief periods. Training children to do even little jobs well takes time. Learning the science behind the methods requires some academic study. For these reasons, this hands-on program in the cafeteria would have to be put in place in stages. All four staffs (academic, janitorial, kitchen, and administrative) would need to plan this program together for it to be workable and to produce good results for the students.

In order to help students learn to not be wasteful with food, we could have secondary students prepare food to be served in the cafeteria under the leadership of a nutritionist, home economics teacher, or competent chef. Vancouver Technical School was doing this some years ago. The course, institutional cooking, proved popular, especially with nonacademic students, and had a waiting list to get into it. Some academic students saw it as a way to get good-paying summer employment at summer camps, nursing homes, private schools, and other such facilities. Of course, they were all learning a life skill.

The purpose of the plan would be to teach respect for those who produce the food and for those who work at the school—for the student to *feel* the importance of this work. It should teach economy instead of waste. One would hope that students would *learn to identify with clean-up jobs* and develop the habit of never leaving a big mess. We could expect that parents and other adults would be pleased to have these responsible, well-mannered children around more often. Children and adults would connect better socially.

Instruction Methods

Information we learn, such as vocabulary, and knowledge we gain through experience is essential to meaningful, progressive thinking. Children cannot think creatively unless they have *learned* the information they need. Furthermore, one cannot think constructively in a vacuum. The child who believes that he or she can is deluding himself with a variant of the idea that the world begins with him or herself and that he or she stands on site on an empty space.

The 2SS will employ a variety of instructional methods to produce well-rounded, knowledgeable, and logical young people. This section discusses the important and controversial topics of language instruction, the use of technology, competition and rewards, as well as critical components of the 2SS—hands-on learning activities and as-needed tutoring.

The Whole Language and Direct Teaching Methods

In our race to be different from the past, and to be up-to-date in education, some of us in the school systems have thrown away some old and useful ideas in favor of new and different ones. We did not want to wait until these new methods were proven more effective. The "leaders" in education convinced many teachers and parents that "new is better than old" and that we were progressive and "on the cutting edge." We now have many children and young adults who have not learned phonics well enough to be able to read words that they have not seen before. Their basic reading skills are wanting.

I do not wish to say that the new ideas and methods that replaced phonics are bad. (It is true that one can also be "too set in one's ways" and become unable to accept any new ideas or methods that could be very beneficial to our children.) These innovations had merit, but we should have kept phonics in the schools. New ideas are still very stimulating in a classroom, but we must be careful to *keep* the methods that have proven their worth over time. Some teachers of children with dyslexia have found that these little people learn to read without much problem when the phonetic sounds are taught first. The 2SS welcomes new ideas like whole language but will not discard old proven methods like phonics.

The *whole language* method of teaching reading, writing, and diction when done correctly, has some very desirable results. However, it is not generally taught – probably because it could not work well in today's large classes. The whole language method is very informal compared with the direct teaching (traditional) method. *Direct teaching* is formal, orderly, organized, and consistent. Primary pupils love predictability. It frees their minds to take in the new lesson. Although experienced teachers are able to handle large classes while teaching with this traditional method, the results are much better in smaller classes, for obvious reasons.

The whole language method *works well only in small classes*. It tries to teach children to read, write, and think by exposing them to good literature (teacher's choice). Children learn first by recognizing a phrase then each word and then, finally, the letters.

These are two opposing philosophies of teaching children to read and write, each of which would seem to exclude the other. Although some teachers would disagree, my own experience tells me that both methods are limited and both are very necessary for good development in learning to use language. The whole language method begins in the home at age two or three, when Mom or Dad reads and tells stories regularly for the children's enjoyment. By the time students are in primary school, they are highly motivated to learn phonics and spelling in the direct learning mode. However, for best results, parents and teachers must continue reading ever more interesting books with these children at home and at school.

Under the best of circumstances, the child from a very early age should have rhymes and stories read to him or her, until about age eight. This child will not know but will be well acquainted with proper (higher level) English. After that, learning phonics, spelling, vocabulary, pronunciation, reading, and writing turns into a lot of fun, because at this point, the child will begin to appreciate the importance of these things.

People who spend much time watching TV are not as competent in expressing ideas as are the readers of library books. To become well educated, one must read many books. Schools that offer their students a good education, have a very good, active library and librarian.

Teachers should be very familiar with *both* approaches. Together, they are highly effective. Both methods would be used in the 2SS.

Technology

With so much attention on technologies, which are being regularly replaced by better models, we hoped that, if we bought enough labor-saving devices, the most up-to-date computers, and the most advanced software, we would surely provide a bright, new future for our children. To date, there is little evidence that new technologies are improving the futures of our young people. There is much evidence to the contrary. The 2SS recognizes both the great good and the tremendous harm that new technology can cause in our children.

Although technology obviously has huge potential for benefiting young people, it also has an equal potential for causing them harm. We are only beginning to realize the great amount of harm that still-developing technology can do to our schoolchildren. The following list shows some of the reasons technology hampers children's ability to learn.

1. It helps us to forget important information. If we do not think about the information that is on the Internet, then it becomes useless clutter.
2. It affects the memory. (People are told that they don't need to remember; the computer will do it.)
3. It takes time away from noticing important relationships, which lead to new ideas, and leave no time to consider why, where, and how.
4. It ignores the changes in the global and local environment (not involved with real life) physical health (obesity, osteoporosis, arthritis, and allergies)
5. Too much daily time on the computer replaces time spent becoming aware of other people's needs (Children's duties, manners, promises, assignments suffer as a result.)
6. Virtual reality displaces reality. (Violence to other people does not shock but seems acceptable, normal, and entertaining.)

Computers store and make available, with just a few key strokes, a superfluity of information. The computer is, however, a seductive tool and can easily take over a child's life, encroaching on time that he or she could spend on concrete, physical activities, such as cooking or making tangible things. In addition, the computer can introduce children to devious behaviors and situations via outside influences, such as pedophilia, online bullying, and other predatory misconduct. The value of the computer is indisputable. The danger of the computer is indisputable. Ongoing monitoring by responsible, caring adults becomes ever more important. The idea is to set students free to become creative and to come up with new ideas. To say that children should not learn to use computers would be unreasonable and would put a child at a great disadvantage in this technical world. The key here is to teach children, when they are very young, to set their own parameters and find a healthy balance between time spent on the computer and time spent participating in other activities. Providing young people with enjoyable experiences early in life gives them more choices. We must ensure that they have these alternatives; otherwise, computer time is threatening to replace the development of creative thinking and the practice of skills, such as drama, dancing, singing, drawing, writing, cooking, sewing, carpentry, and the like. But a balance can be found by integrating computer usage and constructive creation. For example, a child might research how to make string jewelry on the Internet and then take the beads and make his or her own amulet.

Within the classroom, technology is great for children when its use is controlled by a competent teacher. It is very damaging, however, when it is used to replace teacher attention, or time with parents. Videos, for example, are extremely effective in small classes if a teacher has time to preview the video and adapt the presentation to the lesson and to the students. In large or combined classes, videos in the school are no better than TV at home. Unless children are challenged, they will watch videos passively and miss much that is worthwhile. Under present learning conditions, overworked teachers often need these methods as a holding device while they get some other important work done. It is, however, a dreadful waste of our children's time. Educators and parents should not accept new teaching tools unless there is strong evidence that they improve student performance.

Activities

When a child participates, he or she is getting experience. An infant learns only through experience at first. Later the baby learns by watching and listening *and* by participating. For example, you offer a baby her bottle and she takes it and enjoys the drink.

In school, one learns to read by reading, to write by writing, to think by working on problems, and to be fair by playing games by the rules. One learns by observation or by listening—*only if* he or she actually participates as well.

From their child's birth until the time he or she reaches school age, parents should be providing the child with a great variety of mostly *pleasant* experiences involving seeing, hearing, and feeling. When children attend primary school, their teachers will often use a hands-on approach to teaching them mathematical concepts, such as counting, adding, subtracting, sizes, shapes, and fractions.

A child's school life should continue to provide him or her with varying interesting activities—in sports, art, music, nature, constructions, cooking, and shopping. From these experiences, it is a small step for children to learn to deal effectively and happily with mathematical concepts like numbers, fractions, proportions, angles, areas, volumes, and speed.

As schools use less and less of the hands-on approach to math, children begin to lose the connection between the theory and the use of math in real life.

Even high school students need to be *shown* how algebra and geometry are used in the work world. Math that students are learning in the morning could be applied in an afternoon activity as, for example: a landscaping project that involves calculating the volume of earth to be ordered and applied to the yard, or any similar real-life project.

The 2SS is designed to help replace the unwanted effects of TV and the like on our children's young minds with very interesting, educational activities. In this system, children would learn about a new topic through physical experiences of interest to them, such as helping with a science experiment. With some physical involvement, math, social studies, and science would make more sense and become interesting to our children.

When we teach theory (in math, science, social studies, language, or any other subject.) we must always make a strong connection between that theory and its practical application. Otherwise, students will soon become bored. Children always become very interested in learning when they can see and feel how the theory they're studying relates to their own real world.

Competent teachers use a variety of methods for first grabbing the attention of everyone in the class, holding it while they teach for a short time, and then requiring responses from individuals in various ways. If the lesson lasts for an hour, the teacher varies the approaches until the new lesson is complete. Methods of excellent teaching vary greatly—especially from teacher to teacher and from subject to subject—when classes are small.

For the lesson to become embedded in the students' minds, successful teachers have at least five ways of reviewing the material learned. These may include

- writing notes and drawing and labeling diagrams;
- discussing key points as a class;
- watching the relevant part of a video;
- reading the text book and answering questions in full sentences (homework);
- studying for the teacher's test;
- writing the test; and
- sending the marked test home with the child to show unhurried parents who have the interest and the time to take a careful look at it (a huge advantage to the children but possible only if the class is small).

To reinforce learning, teachers may have the students see, hear, touch, ask, discuss, answer, argue, compare, combine, read, write, and use references. These are all important methods used in good teaching. There is no comparison between the versatility of a good teacher and the limitations of the computer when it comes to comparing teaching methods.

Good methods turn children into eager learners. Children, by their behavior, can tell you if they are receiving effective teaching. Lessons, solidly learned, help to build self-confidence and a willingness to do assignments.

Under our present school system myriad hands-on activities are not possible because of the constraints of time and facilities. The 2SS is a plan that motivates children to learn by using extra time and space for interesting hands-on experiences. School, in the afternoons, would be concerned, in large part, with providing students with various activities and experiences to help them feel and appreciate the connection between reality and academic learning. They will be interested because the lesson has meaning for *them*. When students *want to know* what they are being expected to learn, they are not bored.

A normal child is naturally cheerful under most conditions—not bored. Boredom would be a symptom of something wrong to be taken seriously in the 2SS. And the *causes* of the symptom would be eliminated. Children who are involved physically, emotionally, and intellectually in a learning exercise are both happy and interested in learning more. Learning what you want to know is nearly always a lot of fun.

With good learning conditions, the 2SS would attract a variety of the most talented teachers with the biggest repertoire of methods that catch and hold the interest of students. With this system, learning would become a very attractive activity for every one of our youngsters in a sustained way.

Tutoring

Tutoring is a natural activity in large families. However, in our country, large families are mostly a thing of the past. Because tutoring is so beneficial to both the tutor and the learner, we should include it in our new 2SS. In the process, both tutor and learner learn the subject matter better, and the social experience helps to develop both involved personalities. Peer tutoring and cross-age tutoring are good, old ideas that should be brought back into the educational system. Under the direction of competent teachers, tutoring would also save time. Peer tutoring could be an enrichment activity for all students.

Some specific ideas for tutoring are as follows:

- Have senior students work with juniors for credit toward graduation.
- Encourage retired teachers to volunteer their time to discuss with and help students who want help.
- Provide a room with discussion cubicles at convenient times and places to accommodate this valuable activity. Any expenses would best be borne by the government.

The 2SS would be inclined to use this method whenever it was obviously beneficial to *both* participants.

Competition

Competition (including standardized testing) is an effective tool if carefully used only once in a while. It can easily be *overused* to the detriment of learning. Overemphasis on testing and other forms of competition can cause

1. the shrinking of learning time;
2. unnecessary anguish, which prevents learning;
3. the practice of cheating;
4. personal dislikes for the subject of study;
5. nastiness, as found in overly competitive games; and
6. use of *the wrong reason* for learning.

This is why competent teachers resist the overuse of standardized tests.

We must be careful to protect the joy of learning in every student by arranging and planning lessons that are not excessively difficult but always fresh with the challenge of a new idea or two.

Competition can also be highly effective when all those involved feel they have a fair chance of doing well. Some competition between near equal adults or students is often very stimulating and positive in results. The habits fostered by healthy competition can later also function among adults in the workplace and result in their superior achievements.

For example, a fellow teacher, Miss Peters, had a PE class of thirty students. She knew how much excitement and fun is possible in basketball when the team players are of near equal strength and skill. She chose two girls to help her choose six teams. The first girl picked the ten best athletes from the class. The second girl chose the weakest ten. And the teacher had the middle group. Then each group divided into two equal, opposing teams that would play against each other. The two best teams played against each other. The two weakest teams challenged each other in a game, while the two teams of middle ability for the game had their own game. All six teams played their competitive games at the same time in the gym. *Everybody enjoyed him or herself. Most were amazed that they thought that the weak teams had the most fun!*

The 2SS is planned so that teachers can be aware of each child's strengths, weaknesses, and interests during lesson preparation, so that success for each child is assured. Healthy, friendly competition develops naturally among small groups of friends.

Another idea that often comes up when discussing competition is the idea of rewards. At school, it may seem like a good idea to offer prizes for outstanding achievement. However, emphasis on competition for a reward may often turn out to be discouraging to the very people you are trying to motivate. In a competition, *there are more losers than winners.* Next time, they will not be very excited about trying.

Ultimately, if competition will be part of the classroom dynamic, teachers should ensure that it is stimulating and rewarding for every student.

Assessment

ALTHOUGH GRADES CAN MOTIVATE some children to do better, they are very often not effective for that purpose. They can be quite neutral for many and really quite discouraging for others.

Children in the primary grades do not need to be distracted from their joy of learning by being pressured in this way to try harder.

Because the 2SS policy involves keeping each child interested and actively involved in all his or her courses, the most important criterion for the success of the student and of the system is how interested and involved children remain in learning. This is not something that is easily measured. Joy is not measured, just as taste is not measured. Perhaps an observation of negative symptoms is more relevant. Negative systems include children acting out or performing at a lesser rate, while positive symptoms include children paying close attention. Test results will be a close second in importance in middle school. The 2SS would have regular report cards with marks and remarks. Parents would be able to tell how well their children are doing in school by the marks and remarks in the report card but also by their child's eagerness every morning to attend school.

It's important to note that, although tests shouldn't be the primary indicator of success for elementary schoolchildren, they are still important and need to be honest and accurate. Parents want to know how well their children are doing compared with others in that grade so they can be aware of their children's strengths and weaknesses and can work with them on problem areas. Children like to know the truth about how they are doing and will lose respect for adults who try to hide it by giving undeserved marks.

In the upper grades, active interest and test results would be seen as equally important in our measure of success. Test results become more important in high school, as these youth prepare in a safe environment for the fair (or unfair) judgments of the adult world.

In June, as our present public schools are nearing the end of the academic year, teachers have a difficult decision to make about whether or not some pupils should "pass" or should repeat the grade. Usually the child concerned has not mastered the reading, writing, or number work. If a student begins the next grade with a deficiency in an academic subject, he or she will be at an enormous disadvantage, especially if the student's study habits are not strong enough for him or her to work twice as hard next year on the weak subject. This is really too much to expect of most elementary students, as teachers will realize. So this child will limp along from grade to grade, never being very proud or confident of his or her accomplishments academically. This is *not* a good situation; it's very damaging to a student's chances to feel successful. If, however, the teacher "fails" the student, he or she may become socially depressed and hate school for that reason. Next year, the other subjects may turn out to be too easy or too boring. The student's work habits, such as they are, could very well suffer further deterioration.

The 2SS is a plan that accommodates the needs of individual students early in the school year. A child who is not mastering the basic concepts or skills in any academic subject would receive regular tutoring for about one hour every afternoon until he or she has learned the concept well enough to do the regular assignments of the class. The 2SS provides for teacher awareness of each student's progress or failure to progress—not later, but while it is happening. Of course, this is not possible in our present public schools with overly large classes.

After the 2SS is well established, the effectiveness of the *teachers* would be judged more by the interest and involvement of students in their learning activities than by their students' marks on tests.

Additional Factors to Consider

The majority of parents, mostly for very good reasons, are seldom involved in school affairs. Yet we all know that children do much better in their academic subjects when they have parents who can and do take the time to meet some of the staff (by going to some school meetings and to organized activities such as concerts, plays, track meets, or open houses). However, some children need much closer attention to their needs in order to give them a good start. Under present circumstances, too many of these children are not getting the understanding and support that would turn them into successful learners.

Each school in the 2SS would probably do well to include several qualified social workers on the staff, who would serve as the following:

- Counselors for students, staff, and parents – Excluding the academic part of the system, social workers should take an active part in helping to plan school programs that involve the physical, mental, emotional, and social well-being of children and teens.
- "Professional parents" (not disciplinarians) – Social workers should help students who are being bullied or need help in organizing themselves for a smoother school day. This kind of service would be most valuable in the primary grades but could be needed at any level. Social workers would be aware of the basic conditioning necessary for each child—conditioning that could lead to better social and academic growth. The social worker would focus on individual children's physical and emotional needs. Has the child eaten? Was the food nutritious? Is he or she dressed comfortably? Is the student being excluded socially by other children? Is he or she overly shy? What are the problems?

The social workers would attempt to make strategic changes—some small and temporary, others large and lasting for individual students. When given the wherewithal, social workers are well aware of how to prevent most of the learning problems that children have at school. They could do more good for society if their work were meant to be preventive rather than stopgap in nature. The 2SS is preventive and positive in purpose. Social workers' expertise and knowledge could be extremely useful, especially during the first ten years of this system.

In addition to social workers, volunteer teachers' aides would benefit students and teachers alike. They reduce school expenses. While it's true that paid teacher aides are more dependable, making lesson planning more successful, volunteers are beneficial in certain capacities. For example, volunteers can help at school concerts, at school sports meets, or on school trips. In these days of cutbacks in education and oversize classes, volunteers can mitigate the situation *if* the teacher *can depend on this free assistance* for months at a time. If volunteers are parents (as they will likely be) they will have the opportunity to observe their own children in the school setting.

Although decreased class sizes would render the 2SS schools more capable of providing timely attention to every schoolchild's needs as he or she is developing through the grades, skilled volunteer aides would still be welcome, and their assistance would be much appreciated by both children and teachers. Their very interest in the children's activities adds strength and direction to the children's enthusiasm for their projects. This kind of contact with adults is very valuable to the individual child.

Chapter 3

How the 2SS Can Brighten Our Future

ALTHOUGH YET UNTESTED, THE 2SS logically supports myriad positive outcomes at individual, as well as corporate, levels. Students, parents, teachers, school administrators, and society at large stand to benefit from the implementation of this new system. This chapter discusses many of the benefits that are likely to arise as results of the 2SS—though keep in mind that these benefits will take time, perhaps years, to emerge.

Advantages for Students

The two-school system is especially suited to children's development, as it focuses on their individual needs—whether they need longer days in care because their parents are in the workforce or just more attention and encouragement in their special talents. Essentially, we can break children's needs into three categories:

1. The physical child needs regular, suitable activities that exercise the muscles. The muscles, organs (including the brain), and bones do not develop well in a child who eats fast foods, watches the screen, or spends hours on the phone daily. The 2SS will address this need by having a free health foods-only cafeteria and small classes so that help from the teacher, when needed, is available most of the time.

2. The thinking child's brain is similar to our set of muscles in that it needs an object (or an idea) to work on. It requires tools (vocabulary, number sense, and information) to do most thinking jobs. It takes practice (lessons and exercises) to develop thinking skills. The "workouts" need to be gradually more difficult and varied to prevent boredom and to enable children to reach a higher level of performance. In general, the brain gets very little challenge when the child is watching television for hours. This situation must be replaced with one that is more favorable to child development. Small classes would be standard in the 2SS. Small classes offer each child more individual interaction with the teacher, thus offering him or her ongoing stimulus, including questions and discussion.

3. The emotional child needs developing. Even a child who has all the advantages except that of the regular company of a loving parent cannot easily develop the ability to love unselfishly. Other emotions that need to be developed are those associated with sharing, patience, protection, kindness, playfulness, and belonging. For this warmth to grow in a young individual, the child needs to be living these experiences daily. The 2SS is poised to address a child's emotional needs more effectively than current school systems because of the dedicated teacher attention in the smaller classrooms. In addition, the atmosphere of a long (and gentler) school day in the 2SS would help to stabilize children's lives most of the week, by providing them with a place where they are free to grow intellectually, socially, and physically.

How a child experiences the major periods of the day—before school, at school, and after school—is very important. How a child uses each of these time blocks is sure to shape the kind of person he or she will become. All three aspects of our makeup—the brain, the muscles, and the visceral feelings—are dependent on a supply of oxygen, water, and food. A pain in the body, no matter the source (be it from a nasty word, an accident, a disease, or overwork) affects all three areas, although not equally. When we consider our responsibility for the development of children, it would be very foolish to ignore any one of the three aspects of growth to maturity—intellectual, physical, and emotional.

The 2SS takes all three into account. It is a plan that provides a child with the time, the teachers, and the accommodation necessary for the development of a healthy, active body; a knowledgeable, thinking mind; and a love for his or her fellow citizens. This plan effectively prevents the unwanted possibilities of development. The sections that follow provide more detail on the myriad ways the 2SS will benefit children in regard to their physical, mental, and emotional well-being.

Invoking Interest in Studies and Preventing Boredom

Why are children and teenagers bored? This answer came from a teenager whom my brother met while in the Netherlands: *"I don't care."*

This response is typical in First-World countries. Although we, parents and teachers, do challenge teens quite often, we are not able to put any kind of real urgency into the challenge. For young people who don't care, there is often no immediate important consequence if, for example, they don't do an assignment or clean the kitchen. For some very good reasons, we no longer use prompt corporal punishment as incentives, and it does not take a psychologist to realize that teens live only in the *immediate* past, in the present, and in the *immediate* future. Although teens can talk about the distant future, it never seems very real or important to them.

Teenagers' friends who have the same habits make this kind of attitude of not caring seem acceptable. The concerned adult is seen as bothersome, tiresome, and boring. And soon after that, for these youngsters, it is time to connect with a friend again. Friends are not boring. They are real. Their friends can be both nice and nasty to them. Friends are interesting because teens interact emotionally with them.

In short, boredom and lack of involvement are closely related:

1. To make a hockey game, a horse race, or even some card games interesting, it seems you have to add betting. Why? To make it more *interesting*! It seems we have a need to feel more *involved emotionally* somehow.
2. Adolescents with "nothing to do" like to wander around in groups. To keep things interesting, they set up tensions, which come in mostly negative forms, such as
   - harassment of other teens;
   - damage to property;
   - shoplifting;
   - robbing vulnerable people;

- daring each other;
- driving dangerously; and
- adventures with drugs, sex, and other illicit behaviors.

Children participate in all of these activities to find emotional involvement and relief from boredom.

On top of this boredom, young people are becoming increasingly distracted and neglected. Technology has had, and is having, its effect on what both adults and children are doing with their time. In general, both parents work in order to have a home, two children, several phones, a vehicle, electrical appliances, special clothes, three TVs, two computers, and credit cards to make shopping easy (and often as out of control as the children). *Things* have become more important than time.

The way children spend their time has changed, too. With school buses, TV's, computer games, cell phones, fast food, and many other modern conveniences, in addition to absent, working parents, children in general have become sedentary. So their bodies are unexcited and tend to do what is easy. It seems that only the presence of peers gives meaning to an activity that requires real effort.

It's important to recognize that *real* learning is not boring; people who are bored are not learning. If a child grows without learning and is "bored," then that child is being neglected and will be ill prepared to deal with the problems, responsibilities, and pleasures of adulthood. Boredom in young people is a sign that we adults are failing to provide suitable challenges that lead to their positive growth. Successful, experienced teachers and most responsible parents know that the years through childhood must be

- carefully structured (to match each young person's interests and abilities) and
- supervised with prompt assistance where needed in order that these children make good use of their precious time.

This kind of involvement can be very uplifting to the student, giving him or her the experience of achievement. And the very fact that the child is achieving success is also uplifting for his teachers and parents. Too much waiting for help destroys a student's enthusiasm for the subject. It is up to us, as adults, to see that our young people are not neglected in this way.

The 2SS is a plan that seriously aims to meet the various needs of each student while still having an all-inclusive registration policy. Successful private schools, like Montessori, limit the number and quality of students that they will accept. Public schools try to accept all children in their school district. Public schools are more democratic and charge no entry fee. If our public schools changed to the Two-School System, all children would be able to enjoy the many advantages this system has for a happier, more successful lifetime.

The 2SS effectively minimizes boredom in favor of the students' *active mental, emotional,* and (whenever possible) *physical involvement* in their own projects.

Before it is too late, we need to wake up to the fact that our children are becoming bored. This should be a wake-up call to teachers and parents. Boredom is not normal for children; it is a sign that something is *wrong.* Children have no time to lose. They need to experience the real world of work and consequences, of physical activity, and of dealing with the problems and joys that contact with nature brings. "Virtual reality" should be a *last* option, because children learn much more from real experience. Nature activates the whole person and causes the child to grow physically, emotionally, spiritually, creatively, critically, and intellectually—often all at the same time. Real-life experience is *much* more valuable to a child's development than is virtual involvement.

The benefits of a small class

In particular, lessons become alive and meaningful to children who are lucky enough to be in a small class where the teacher can involve each child in real-life activities that relate to the skill or theory he or she is teaching. Learning through new, meaningful experiences is what being young is all about. Children of all ages are easy to lead, to teach, and to involve. Everything is new and interesting to them.

But when we put children in large classes and in large schools where "one size fits all," we force them into situations that are unsuitable for very many students. Teachers know that, when a school is very large and classes are comprised of more than twenty-four students, it becomes close to impossible for a teacher to make lessons that reach the interests of *all* individual students and impossible to assign work that isn't *too easy* for some and *too hard* for others. In either, school is boring and students do assignments less effectively. The class size of the 2SS, at ten to twelve students for K to 3 and twenty to twenty-four students for grades

4 to 12, enables teachers to effectively engage every single student in the curriculum.

With bigger schools, many children also have long, unavoidable bus rides, where the boredom would continue if it weren't for the energetic clowns among them or, more often, the "bullies" who need to remind everyone of their superior place in the pecking order, at the expense of regularly harassing some unfortunate student.

Children today continue to attend school mainly because it is compulsory. Because of the smaller classes of 2SS, which would allow teachers to pay attention to each child's individual needs, these problems should not be an issue in the 2SS. Children would not want to miss any school days while they had the 2SS.

Sharing

The advantages of enjoying hands-on learning

To have a healthy, well-balanced life, all people should have fun periodically. However, children require (as part of their development) more enjoyment than adults do. An adult is fortunate if his or her life's work is very interesting to him or her. A child's work needs to be interesting, even enjoyable, in order for the child to learn what he or she needs to know.

Childhood is a time of finding out about the world, mostly through play. But, you say, school is not play; education isn't always fun, and it takes work. Actually, what children do in school is something between play and work. It is called "learning." Adults work, mostly because they have to. But when adults work for fun, they call it a hobby.

Children practice skills and take on new experiences and knowledge, which is both work and fun. What children do in school often requires intense concentration and effort. They are developing through their learning. It is *boredom* that is so burdensome to healthy, active children. Drills (lessons with changing repetition) can be great fun, or they can be painful. If the lessons are not too difficult and not too easy, but new and slightly changing, then the children will enjoy the challenges. These children will tell you that school is fun.

A consistently unhappy child does not learn well, although an occasional bad day can be a valuable learning experience. However, if a child regularly does not wish to be at school, you can be pretty certain that the child is not benefiting educationally when he or she is at school. The child could be suffering from some difficulty, such as lack of sleep, poor eyesight, unnoticed bullying, other undisclosed fears, hunger, wearing the wrong clothes, or attempting lessons that are too easy or too hard.

If a child is well prepared and cheerful when he or she leaves for school in the morning, then we can guess that school is a stimulating happy place, and that the child may be learning as expected. The 2SS would try to keep children and teachers happy by improving learning conditions with smaller classes and more varied, challenging activities throughout the school day under the guidance and protection of qualified staff. Because classes in the 2SS will be small and manageable, children will waste less time while waiting for their turn to talk with the teacher. This eliminates opportunities for bullies to harass the shy kids. Instead, all children will feel free to learn—including the now former bullies—and the former shy kids will begin to feel welcome as participating members of the group.

***

The need for stimulation applies to teenagers too. When teens feel they have no useful role to play in society, they become bored and unchallenged. Their unused surplus of energy wants a release, and it sometimes finds its expression in vandalism, fighting, or bullying. Healthy young people have a natural desire to be physically active and to try new adventures. A good teacher does not usually suppress this urge but, instead, steers the energy into learning through experience where possible. Hands-on learning and sports are examples of this.

When classes are small, teachers can be accomplish much by having students participate in an activity that illustrates a point, allowing the class to see the connection between the lesson and reality. For example, teachers could take a class on a short hike to show them examples of what they learned in the book. Students with strong muscles *crave* to be active, while physically weaker students *need* to be active and so students should be involved, physically if possible, in activities that reinforce the lessons. This is how they learn willingly. Listening to the teacher or reading the textbook is a part of school learning. When actually learning, the student is doing something *with* the information—answering or asking questions, working on a project, discussing, researching, comparing, or preparing a presentation for the class—in order to feel the sense of it.

In addition to providing positive incentives for participating in learning, the 2SS will avoid canceling out children's learning with negative activities (as previously mentioned in this book). In this system, their learning will be regularly reinforced in many ways. Reinforcement may include a related real life experience, thus giving students heightened interest as they progress.

The incentive of healthy, positive peer pressure
For a child, peer pressure is often stronger than pressure from teachers or parents. Reduced contact with parents or teachers because of large classes and busy lives can easily leave the child more open for peer pressure.

Children feel very strongly that, in order to be accepted by a certain group, they must look, act, and talk like the members of that group. For children, peer pressure and adult pressure, more often than not, run counter to each other. It is, therefore, confusing and unsettling to a child who is living with two contradictory pressures on him.

Children are happiest when they know what they can or cannot do. When boundaries restricting their behavior are well established, kids become free to concentrate on learning new skills and ideas. Children best learn social boundaries from the influence of *adults*.

If parents and teachers do not establish boundaries around negative behaviors and control the influences on their children, then they may be sure that someone else (such as bullies) will—especially if they do not have time to notice. We could *replace* these regular, unwanted peer pressures by setting boundaries around students' time and keeping them engaged in a variety of stimulating hands-on activities, in close connection with teachers, which is a key attribute of the 2SS.

Peer pressure isn't always negative, however; it *can* have desirable results. Positive peer pressure kicks in when children are and have been consistently guided by adults who understand what they are trying to achieve and how to best do so. Experience and qualifications are equally important.

Peer pressure is an extremely useful tool in teaching children good habits and attitudes, and the benefits are multiplied when things really go right. A *climate* of attitude and behavior is developed in the classroom when the teacher can effectively use his or her influence to set it. This climate serves all levels from K to twelve. If started early and kept consistent, the results are *extremely good*.

Teachers are well placed to use peer pressure to get desired results when learning conditions are right, as in the proposed 2SS. With the influence of positive pressures, children

- do homework without delays;
- feel free to ask questions when things are not clear;
- regularly do their best work;
- have fewer distractions from the learning situation;
- are in the habit of using good manners;
- tidy up after each job or assignment;
- use good English and speak clearly;
- have respect for teachers, parents, and each other;
- feel they are successful and, therefore, feel like trying;
- have good feelings between students and teachers and kids and parents;
- spend less money on clothes and toys;
- spend less time arguing, watching TV, playing computer games, and acting out on frustrations;
- have good routines, which result in better health; and
- are more supportive of each other in difficult times.

The results of positive peer pressure used effectively are efficiency and happiness combined, while desirable progress is achieved in both home and school.

Bringing Balance to Education with Real-World Experience

As discussed in the previous section, children, by their nature, need to be active. Having them sitting while reading, writing, listening, and working on the computer is very important, but whenever possible, we should get them out their chairs to learn by actively experiencing a process or a situation, under the guidance of a sympathetic, experienced teacher. This method of teaching keeps children interested and happy, and they have a better chance of feeling connected to the world of work.

The 2SS is set up to involve children in interesting activities that will give them experience, as well as book learning. They will not need to ask, "Why do I have to learn math, social studies, or science? Why do I have to learn how to use the dictionary?" Their practical, hands-on afternoon activities will help them appreciate the importance of what they are learning. This is a way they learn with more enthusiasm.

Several examples of such activities in the 2SS are as follows:

- Tutoring students of the same grade or younger
- Helping serve food in the cafeteria
- Helping in the cafeteria by clearing the tables
- Refereeing at a game or keeping score
- Helping in the school garden
- Helping to maintain the landscaping
- Working for an hour at the day care if there is a day care close to the school
- Cleaning up the schoolyard with classmates
- Planning and decorating for a school party and cleaning up after the party
- Organizing and managing a student election
- Working with the yearbook committee

The above activities are all forms of hands-on learning. They are purposeful and, therefore, meaningful. These activities help children become good citizens.

Giving students Personal Attention and Nurturing

Before a child can make good progress in his or her development at home or at school the youngster must be free of emotional or social problems, which is the direct result of conscious, healthy child care. Children who leave home for school in a positive frame of mind will be much more open to experiencing new lessons and doing their best work than children who have been emotionally disturbed by unfriendly classmates, scolding parents, or critical or negative teachers. We, as adults, can probably empathize with children in the latter category. Imagine, for example, that our boss yelled at us, after which we sat down to attend to some new and complicated task. We probably would have a hard time doing this well. Children are even more vulnerable to emotional upsets, as they are expected to do something new nearly every day. Such children's ability to think is likely to be severely impaired. Emotionally disturbed children are in no condition to work on a math problem, learn new material, or produce anything creative. Only when a child is physically, emotionally, and socially comfortable is he or she ready to take on new challenges.

Children's personalities are shaped, to a large extent, by the care they received, or did not receive, while growing up. "Kindergarten" means *garden of children*. Good gardeners take great interest in and care of their plants, and the results are gratifying. Good child care is achieved only if caregivers (parents, teachers, coaches, babysitters, and supervisors) give individual children time, paying attention to the child's feelings, interests, and safety. Children cannot grow into caring people, if they are neglected in this respect. When adults are too busy to realize a child's difficulties measuring up to expectations, children learn ways of hiding their personal problems (feelings) from people who seem not to care.

The education system of fifty or sixty years ago did work fairly well for most children in the public schools. Communities consisted mostly of one or two cultures. The upbringing know-how followed well-known, traditional, consistent methods. A large, unrecognized workforce, among other things, nurtured and trained little children.

My own experience as a child can exemplify this, and I will add that my experience at that time was actually pretty typical. At home, while the boys regularly brought fuel for cooking and heating into the house and did some livestock care, their sisters helped their mother in the kitchen and garden or looked after the baby. And sometimes, everybody helped in the garden or with feeding the animals. By the time children were in their teens, they were able to do most of the jobs very well. I was always near my mother or older sisters, observing and participating in jobs to my level. When I was eleven, my mother had her ninth child. My big sister was out working for a wage for a farmer's wife. So my job was to make the meals, wash some clothes, and look after a younger brother and three little sisters for the next five days. After that, Mom could resume her duties.

Although I was young, I (as with most children of that age) had already had some experience so that I could take on so much responsibility for a short time. This made our transition to adulthood just that much easier. I do not advocate going back to the sexist roles in the family; nor does technology suit many of the activities of that day. However, the lesson is that we can, as adults, still be great role models for our children if we maintain close and friendly connections with them.

The "large, unrecognized workforce" that "nurtured and trained little children," has all but disappeared. It is not my role in this book to argue that these nurturers deserved recognition. Rather, we need to look for answers to fill a void in our children's world. This is the purpose of the 2SS.

Cool School

Unfortunately, our "garden of children" (the school) today shows large areas of weeds and evidence of uneven watering, producing too few productive graduates.

How a child feels about school is too often not considered important by a parent or a teacher or by government—at the expense of proper child development. For example:

- Parents are preoccupied with their careers, their business, or their own social lives.
- Teachers teach "subjects," whether too strictly or too lackadaisical, instead of teaching *children*.
- Governments put children in large, impersonal schools with large classes and have children regularly travel long distances on school buses to save money on education.

A large school that has to neglect some of the children is a sad example of unfairness to the innocent. Children learn to accept these harsh learning conditions, and the results are negative for the children's future. Classes are so large that teachers must ignore a child's emotional or physical pains or postpone giving them attention because she or he has a large class to teach.

Additionally, if the teacher is suffering from some negative feelings (like depression, anger, pain, or insecurity) effective interaction with the student will be impaired. Teachers need to establish a positive, pleasant atmosphere that suggests a passion for the subject and a kindly attitude toward each child.

For proper development, children need to feel that parents, teachers, principals, and coaches care about them, which is best achieved on an individual, personal level. Before and at the time of entering school, a child is unique in many subtle ways. From the day a child is born he or she is an individual in that he or she is genetically different from all other individuals. After five years of interacting with home and family, children have even more differences. Being different individuals, they can each learn different things from the same lessons, or they can learn the same things in their own, different ways. Children should be recognized and appreciated for who they are. Technology does not help very much here. What we need is small classes in small schools and teachers who love children so that each child's interests and talents and hopes and fears can be recognized. When a teacher understands what each child is likely to get from a lesson, she can plan some very effective learning situations for each and *every* child.

"Problem children" are often those who are being criticized for being any or a few of the following—lazy, wasteful, self-centered, bored, unfair, impatient, disorganized, antisocial, dishonest, dangerous, erratic, overweight, extreme, unsanitary, immature, careless, underachieving, noncommunicative, angry, or destructive. These unfortunate individuals, who are performing below expectations and who are being blamed for their lack of effort, are usually in no position to improve their ways. Punishing them is *not* going to help them. The cause of the problem lies deeper and calls for some intelligent, sympathetic understanding.

The symptoms of child neglect are in all those adjectives—lazy, wasteful, self-centered, and on and on. When we neglect to recognize the importance of the nurturing, the training, the teaching, the caring, and the respectful recognition that children must have for proper development, then we will naturally have these very bad results.

We mistakenly blame young people for their lack of positive development. Looking at the problem more closely, one can see that it is the home, the school, and society that have failed these young people. Kids need a *closer* connection with parents and other responsible adults in order to develop into good citizens. We have been too preoccupied to notice that our present system is producing these many "problem teens."

The 2SS could be a major part of the solution. We must stop blaming the children. The fault is in our system. It is no longer working, because conditions for raising children have changed enormously. Children have no power to change the situation. They have no voice in our democratic system; nor can they always know what is best for themselves. If this is still a democratic country, then we, the citizens, can make a change worthy of our beloved children.

The 2SS recognizes that each child is unique and that, for good educational growth, classes and schools must be small. The 2SS is a plan that deals with the emotional problems of a child *before* expecting to see academic or other learning to take place. It is a plan that, in the end, produces young adults who care deeply about the people they know. The 2SS will endeavor to make a child feel welcome, respected, and wanted *before* he or she is expected to learn or work on lessons. This would be achieved through good working conditions for both children and teachers. There would be much more positive interaction between teachers and pupils, making for some very good learning results.

The 2SS also recognizes the necessity for a measure of privacy in the working day in order to facilitate self-reflection and mental and physical restoration. Private time is a time to rest, recover, and think. It is a quiet time in which one can reorganize his or her plans or attitudes. All the paid workers and the children should have privacy when they need it, but especially the younger students. To develop into a physically and mentally healthy person one needs a measure of safe, comfortable privacy that one can count on. Primary children should be allowed to rest lying down, as is customary in some kindergarten classes, for regular, short sessions.

The 2SS would achieve this effect with its emphasis on

- reliable, educationally effective routines;
- respect and safety;
- a quiet library;
- a sick room; and
- washrooms with private conditions. (A child who cannot count on having privacy is an abused child, and his or her ability to benefit from the school would be compromised.)

Addressing Academic Needs Early On

The primary grades are important for building the foundations necessary to acquire a good education. Although most school systems agree with the above statement, the 2SS is organized to take the idea *more* seriously. In the Two-School System *all* children must learn to read and write so well in grade one that, when they begin grade two, they are ready to learn grade two reading and writing with *confidence*. Tests do not assess the children's capability well, especially at these tender years. Checkups from teaching supervisors (superintendents or inspectors) can quickly show if a child is reading fluently enough to manage the beginning of the grade two work.

The 2SS would help students from low-income homes and those not familiar with English by providing extra learning time during the library periods. This would be true for learning arithmetic as well. Grade one is as important to a child's future as the foundation is to a tall building. Just the same, effective help should be available to each and every student in *any* grade.

However, the lower the grade in which a child begins to get proper attention to his or her special needs, the greater is the child's success in learning now and later.

Waiting is dead time. Dead time is negative to one's well-being and to one's interest in a topic. Sometimes, waiting is necessary, but the younger the student, the less time he or she should be expected to wait.

A child in grade one should get help at the time it is needed. Although this is good for all grades, it is imperative for the very young. A school is more effective when teachers have time to mark assigned work within a few hours or days, rather than within a few weeks. Often, this is not possible, especially for English, social studies, and literature because of the large number of students in each class and the amount of written work necessary for these subjects.

A school that requires students to wait too long and too often is inefficient; it is burdened with discipline problems and with children who, then, hate school.

The 2SS takes care of this problem in the following ways:

- By reducing class sizes, so that children do not have too much waiting time (during which they tend to lose interest in the particular topic they are studying)
- By establishing pupil competence in the basics early in the primary grades, thus enabling students to use books and other resource material (from grade four up) for their source of information, rather than always having to wait for someone's help, allowing them to develop initiative while getting away from overdependence on other people
- By having a librarian and a library with interesting new books added once a year

Children in the 2SS learn to become independent learners who know how to progress in their studies because they can use books while they wait for personal attention from a teacher. These students do not become bored; nor do they become a problem.

Teaching Responsibility, Discipline, and Consistency

Most of us do not like to admit it, but sometimes we do worry that discipline is a growing social problem. When people in higher positions in the education system tell us that discipline is really quite good and that it is getting better, it makes concerned people worry even more.

Three generations ago, raising children to be disciplined was not the big problem it is today. It is only in the last thirty or forty years that children have had quite so much free time, devoid of responsibility and work. Before that, most children helped mother, father, brother, or sister as soon as they were able and became very proud helpers. It was part of the joy of living then. By the time they were thirteen, they could be responsible for and take pride in accomplishments in *many* of the "adult chores." The change from childhood to adulthood was not as traumatic for them as it is for our teens today.

The reason for this difficult transition is that too many young people today are not learning how to do housekeeping for a family or for themselves. Most of their out-of-school time is free of responsibilities or of work experience. We, parents, supply them with spending money, toys, much time for TV and computer games, and phones for talking to friends. We even make their beds and clean their rooms sometimes. They become very unhappy when parents cannot afford to buy clothes and toys that are as up-to-date as those of their friends. They have very little experience in responsibility to people other than to their peers, who can also be very unreasonable in their demands. On top of these changes, the difference between work and play in our homes and schools has been blurred. We have tried to make work for our children so pleasant and exciting that very little disciplined effort is required of the child.

Under these circumstances, children naturally get quite a distorted picture of the world; they see it as a place where adults are there to fulfill their demands. It is hard for them to feel or notice how unfair it is to their parents, because children are seldom required to do a fair share of the chores. They are not experienced in this area of living and do not feel they should (suddenly) be expected to do work around the home when their friends don't seem to be required to do chores.

This irresponsibility doesn't affect only our young people (and their parents) though. It also affects their progeny. A large number of babies these days are born to teenagers who had not planned them—but who have an initial desire to keep the babies, not realizing that raising a child requires much work and responsibility. They are not prepared to be responsible parents. You may have seen a high school graduation ceremony where the graduate passes her baby to Granny while going up to collect the awards she has won. What award does Granny get? This is not good for the coming generation. The grim truth is that, by giving our children a carefree childhood, we are developing childish adults—and the cycle continues, one generation after another.

Because this pattern is so common, it is difficult or impossible for a small group of parents (or teachers) to change it. When parents or teachers try to lecture children about the past or the future, they are wasting their time and energy. The natural way to grow up is to learn the little consequences of one's mistakes or misdeeds as one goes. Children are not able to think much beyond the present. They should be told no more than twice why certain jobs or rules are necessary. Big rewards, such as an expensive, small car, or dire punishments, such as canceling a planned ski trip to a special resort for not succeeding, are overkill and do not work well. Although corporal punishment can be highly effective and economical, our teachers and parents are not sufficiently familiar with this skill and the psychology involved in the successful use of this method. We have seen too many horrible examples of its misuse. The 2SS does not include corporal punishment because, with good working conditions for all those who are found in this setup, students will require far less and much milder disciplining.

Small rewards and mild consequences are sufficient, but they should be immediate to be effective.

By neglecting to reinforce positive, responsible behaviours and providing suitable, immediate, mild consequences for our children's mistakes, we are denying them a basic start in their education. Teachers and principals are working on this problem quite regularly and often until they become exhausted of time and energy. They have many proactive solutions, which are excellent and highly effective, *provided* there are enough adults with time and energy to make these worthwhile ideas really work.

As anyone with any real-world adult experience knows, even a very clear plan cannot work until we have the time and person power (supportive parents, increased qualified teaching staff, and informed students), which comes down to more money for public education. We need a proactive solution that includes the necessary leaders with the time and the enlightened tax-payers with the money—enlightened in that they can see that avoiding trouble is less expensive than troubleshooting. High quality training and schooling, in the end, costs less in both money and in frustrating results.

The 2SS is such a plan. Teachers would have smaller classes and more time and space to prepare more effective lessons. Individual children would be recognized for their interests, abilities, and efforts. And the length of the school day would allow less time for aimless and often troublemaking behavior. Parents would be able to do their part, confident that their children would be *cheerfully engaged in activities* that will help them become responsible, industrious, educated citizens.

Among the first things that children need to learn when they come to school is how to behave at school. The teacher needs to be able to give instruction to the whole class much of the time, as well as give direction to individuals. The school must have its own order, especially in the classroom. First, children should be taught what to do, and later, they should learn why. (With adults it is better the other way around.) When discipline is good, it becomes possible for all children to learn without frustration. On the other hand, having an unruly child in the classroom is a serious matter because it does cancel some of the learning. If not controlled immediately, the child can destroy the learning atmosphere completely. The unfortunate child who is not fitting into the situation most likely does not deserve punishment but rather some friendly training in following a few rules.

Class discipline is essential to good learning. Therefore, it should be established in grade one and consistently maintained throughout the grades. This is easier to achieve in the 2SS for two important reasons:

1. The system offers a favorable pupil teacher ratio, which means smaller classes and usually results in the joy of learning.
2. The rules of order learned in the morning classes will not be cancelled by unruly behavior in the afternoon. Instead, proper behavior will be reinforced by the order that is necessary to achieve success in hands-on projects in the afternoon. The students would *want* classes to be orderly, because they all love to succeed.

Primary teachers have the job of establishing in their pupils good learning habits. They can do so very well when they get reasonable support from parents and the administration. With favorable working conditions, all good teachers will enjoy well-disciplined classes, especially after the 2SS becomes well-established, which may take a year.

If the class is not too large, one teacher will be able to train and teach at the same time. If we have several poorly behaved children in the same class, then we have a case of overload. If the administration can do nothing about the problem of overload, then the problem will fester. If the problem is "solved" with drugs such as Ritalin, the child's health is being put at risk. It should be obvious that the class is in need of better learning conditions.

It's important to teach responsibility at home, too, so the transitions between home and school are seamless.

Responsibility in a six-year-old is a combination of caring for somebody or something and voluntarily doing the right thing. Exercises to develop responsibility that a child can accomplish at home (and in some measure at school) include the following:

- Caring for the cat or dog—remembering to feed the pet at regular times
- Caring about his or her own health, by doing things like remembering to brush his or her teeth morning and evening and wash his or her hands often
- Looking after his or her schoolbag and contents as an established, regular habit

Responsibility exercises for an eight-year-old might include the following:

- Practicing good habits – For example, a responsible student obtains permission when borrowing something, takes good care of the item, and returns it in a reasonable time and in good condition
- Thinking independently (on the basis of reliable knowledge) – A responsible student is able to think not only of his or her own needs but, at times, also of the needs of others. He or she should be able to help him or herself and others to some extent. For example, when a responsible student is in class, he or she cooperates in the learning situation; contributes constructively to the discussion; and helps with physical arrangements of things, people, and time.
- Exercising some initiative – When a child gets his or her homework done *without* much reminding, it tells us that the child thinks of what he or she should do and has the habit of doing it.

The influence of home and school in developing responsibility (or the lack thereof) is dependent upon the timeliness and consistency of the care and treatment of any particular child. This kind of new progress is, at first, very vulnerable to opposing influences. To establish new, desirable behavior, teachers need to see that the child practices the behavior again soon after he or she first demonstrates it.

Regularity is also part of teaching responsibility. Ultimately, the more consistent the training, the less punishment is necessary. Explanations for rules do not require endless repetition. However, to begin with, understanding how the child feels and thinks, takes time and loving patience. One should take the time to see and listen to what the child says, thinks, and feels. The 2SS accommodates the positive needs of all children in a welcoming, reasonable, consistent manner. Consistency of treatment from the very beginning makes punishment mostly unnecessary.

In order to learn responsibility, children need to *feel* responsible, *practice* responsibility, and *think* with a caring attitude. This is a big daily job—more than is possible for most parents, who already have too much stress from trying to earn a living. The 2SS is in session from 8:00 a.m. to 5:00 p.m., Monday to Friday, for grades one through three—long enough to help children develop responsible habits, and long enough so that other influences are weak enough that they will not cancel the desirable habits of thinking, feeling, and behaving responsibly. For this reason, we need the 2SS.

Instilling Structure and Routine

The human body does well in an established routine for eating, sleeping, working, playing. The body that is on a routine can keep fairly well in spite of bad food or an uncomfortable bed. Routine helps not only the body function better, but also the mind. Conversely, lack of an established routine in the week of a child brings on poor health, bad nerves, and lower achievement at school.

The more educated you are, the more you *know* about order, but the more trained you are the more orderly you *are*. Well-planned routine, good health, and superior effort in schoolwork all tend to reinforce each other. A mature, responsible, dependable person knows much about laws and rules. An infant begins to learn about order when he is put on a feeding, bathing, and sleeping schedule. On the first day of school, the teacher explains and shows the children the times and places for people and things. The next few days are for training. They are learning *order* as they work, play, and come to and leave school.

Since about 1960, the word "training" was dropped from the more advanced educational jargon. Training was for dogs and horses, but not for people. However, half of a good education is training. An educated person cannot function very well in the adult world unless he or she is also trained in how to live near other people without annoying them in one way or another. There are many rules of social behavior that are just part of one's upbringing. These rules become a set of habits.

People who are used to order have noticed how much easier it is for them to get work done. Orderly people get more good work done in less time. They also enjoy the fruits of their labor more, as well as their leisure time. However, although civilization has made tremendous progress in science and technology, by and large, it has yet to find out how to balance work with leisure. During childhood, one should be taught knowledge and skills needed for both work and play, so that, later as an adult, one would have the inclination to do both in a balanced way.

Unfortunately, though, some would-be good students live in chaotic homes, where Mom and Dad are trying to maintain a job and/or social life that uses up nearly all their time and attention. These kids feel the pressure, the necessity of getting their homework done, but are prevented from doing it because they have no regular place or time for this kind of study. When adults are not present, they cannot transmit their values, interests, and attitudes to these students. While parents are fully involved with meeting all kinds of responsibilities, their children are on free time and are looking for exciting amusements where there is no urgency to get any kind of work done.

When they leave high school, graduates are suddenly expected to be good workers and to pay sustained attention to a task. Although our young people mean well and are quite tough in other ways, they are not used to the pressure of working like an adult at home or in the workplace or even at college or university. The 2SS is structured to develop in children the ability to meet the pressures that go along with the disciplines of learning academic, practical, and social lessons. Passing into adult life would seem more gradual and less traumatic than it is for many young people today. Building self-confidence by learning to deal with pressure is an important part of a solid education.

Social interactions are also affected by individuals' abilities to incorporate structure into their daily lives. When two people who are well trained in tidiness and order share a house or a room, they are likely to get along well. However, untidy, disorganized people do not mesh well with other people for long. After they are grown up, they suffer much more from the consequences of their sloppiness, because they no longer have parents to pick up after them. By this time, their bad habits are long-standing, and to change a whole set of habits is nearly impossible. These people should have been trained *early* in life. Structure is what is missing most in the lives of our young people now. Their out-of-school learning is too haphazard and also needlessly dangerous. Much of their free-time learning is not very useful (like studying hairstyles and watching TV) and even harmful (like practicing their bullying skills and trying drugs) during this unstructured time. The purpose of structure in a child's day is to provide a plan to facilitate his or her best possible development.

Without structure, all the other positive things in a child's life—good methods of teaching, extra patience, careful counseling, and wise parenting—seem to fail to a noticeable extent. Teaching becomes extremely inefficient at home and at school without structure. It is important that everyone has some idea of what to expect at different times of the day, week, or year.

A school system with structure is one that has definite rules and limitations. All institutions, including schools, need structure. All communities also need rules and limitations. Rules and limitations do not exist without their matching consequences when carelessly disregarded. Far too many schoolchildren today cannot read and write well enough to do their homework properly. Structure is a great help when teaching language skills (and most other subjects).

Order in a school is like oil in a smooth-running engine. Desks, books, supplies, and students must be in the right places before efficient learning can take place. A good timetable properly followed makes for an established routine. Routine makes it possible to take the repetitive part of the schoolwork for granted, thereby freeing teachers and students to proceed to the more interesting parts of their work or activity.

There is more "freedom" for more children when adults provide a structured, protected choice of activities for each day. When children are not wasting time looking for missing items or being worried about threats from bullies, they can enjoy trying new skills, like skating, playing ball, acting, singing, homework, gymnastics, discussing ideas, and making new friends.

The 2SS frees the children to enjoy learning without the frustrations that usually go with unplanned or unprotected time. Children need choices from among many structured activities to maintain their interest throughout the afternoons. Children need order with choice—just as adults do. Children thrive when there is both choice and order.

The 2SS, although quite flexible, is a serious attempt to put better structure back into our children's lives. Children need to know better what to expect. The 2SS is a framework built on well-established routine, to be filled with positive, exciting, new lessons.

The 2SS includes training in orderly living, as well as education in the academic subjects. It endeavors to teach children:

1. To work willingly and to feel the pleasant sense of serious accomplishment
2. To feel that there is a time and a place to enjoy recreation, improving motor skills in the company of new and old friends
3. To appreciate quiet time, when deep thinking can become a habit, as in the library or after going to bed (early enough)

It is our responsibility to see that the children of today are not burdened with patterns of harmful behavior as they enter their adulthood and find that they have missed learning the ordinary skills of living. They would be right in blaming us older folks for their unnecessary handicap. This situation, however, is changeable with a constructive school system.

Providing Continuity and a Sense of Belonging

Since the 1960s, support from relatives has become less and less prevalent, as many families no longer live in communities made up of many relatives. Grandparents no longer see much of their grandchildren as they grow up. Families have become very small. Nowadays, many marriages do not last through child raising. Single-parent families have become common, and most of them are headed by the mother, who also works for an income to pay the bills. She has little time left to enjoy the company of her kids and to see to their emotional needs.

Most young families today must rent because they cannot afford to buy a home. This affects how long they stay in the community, which affects their identity with their new community. And it affects their necessary knowledge of the dangers and the advantages of the new area. In order for parents to have more influence on the direction of their children's development, they would have to spend *much* more regular time communicating with their kids—and under more positive circumstances.

We know that the feeling of belonging with a group of people, which is the result of continuity, is extremely important, especially to children. Consider culture, for example. Any culture is the result of consistency over many generations. Like the well-established, effective habits of a person, culture is the result of methods that have worked successfully over many generations. Culture provides rhythm and direction—a kind of automation that has freed people for generations to deal with new joys or with solving the problems of living. In early childhood, children need an environment of consistency, of harmony, and of very few physical or emotional problems. This is the time when they must get comfortably acquainted with their immediate world. As they become physically and mentally more able, they add to their experience and knowledge. The "what" and "how" of their learning is colored by the culture. Culture provides comfort, consistency, and continuity—all essential to good development.

Continuity in children's development, in addition to cultural identity, involves having the same home, the same parents, and the same school system over the years. In an age of international commerce and company employment, though, it is difficult for a family to rely upon being in a permanent home, having the same school, or maintaining community connections. It is hard to develop in our young people good habits of order, of health, of manners, and of study.

Schools are well positioned to provide a counterbalance to the lack of continuity in many children's personal lives. With continuity, teachers and students do not lose their aim or purpose. The curriculum should also have continuity built into the courses of study, so as to reinforce what students have learned and avoid the boredom of repetition. The core of the curriculum should be as widespread geographically as possible, to make for better continuity for the students who must move. A sense of camaraderie with other students of all ages lends to this sense of belonging as well; therefore, older students should, if possible, help younger ones in their studies, wherever tutoring situations can be comfortably arranged. This connection between younger and older children helps students find their place in the continuity of education in a changing society as is highly educational to both learner and tutor. Small schools in small communities, both of which are trademarks of the 2SS, have most of these advantages.

When classes are not large, students enjoy discussing with each other and with their teacher the new ideas that arise in their lessons. Everyone is part of the discussions. Everyone belongs to the group, including the teacher. Students feel recognized and welcome. It is somewhat like a large family where the people like to see you do your best. This sense of belonging breeds enthusiasm or school spirit.

In a school with positive spirit, the place is neither quiet nor noisy. It is not overly tidy; nor is it messy. The atmosphere is cheerful, industrious, and cooperative. In this place, things may go wrong quite often—but *never* for long. When students share that comfortable feeling of belonging with the others in the school, it shows outwardly as school spirit. It is the *obvious* mark of a successful school. In the 2SS, each school would be judged by the strength of its school spirit.

Nurturing Cooperative Relationships

Lately, society has been moving away from peace, not toward it. Some of us are becoming people with limited tolerance for those who are different. Children come to see violence as a way of solving all kinds of problems quickly and simply. This causes children to become extremely difficult to reason with. Instead of learning from responsible adults how to be thoughtful, constructive, cooperative, and understanding of other people, they are learning to have little patience with their problems and remain mentally ill-equipped to meet the challenge. This tendency does not bode well for society—even in our immediate future.

Intelligent cooperation is the stuff of a successful workplace and also that of a democratic society. Unfortunately, learning a peaceful way of living is much more involved (more complicated) than is learning a violent way. Cooperation, care, sympathy, understanding, and appreciation of other people require a much higher level of thinking than do hate, revenge, and fighting. Building a house, a farm, or a business; raising a family; or developing an education system are all endeavors that require much thoughtful planning; careful, honest work; and cooperation at a high level over a long period of time.

It naturally follows, then, that children should learn how to work harmoniously with others as well as by themselves. Teachers should encourage children to help each other, and they should teach this cooperation in all activities. Cooperation includes respect for others, good intercommunication, patience, consideration, helpfulness, and thoughtfulness. These qualities should become imbedded in the children's habits and attitudes by the time they are ready to leave school. Obedience is not the same as cooperation. Cooperation is, properly, a two-way process between equals; it's not about following orders, as with obedience. Everyone must be heard.

Students can learn and maintain skills in cooperation much better in an uncrowded, friendly, interesting place, as in a 2SS classroom. Today's classrooms are too crowded and too impersonal for good, successful discussions. We need to improve our schools so that teaching this skill to all students, as proposed in the 2SS, will become possible.

When more adults realize that children *must* have an appropriate opportunity to voice themselves (as in cooperation), then we can begin to hope for a more constructive future.

Supporting Healthy Lifestyles

These days, it is too easy for children and adults to get used to living with habits that harm their health. Our modern way of living discourages children from being physically active. The car and the school bus take our children where they need or want to go. Walking or cycling has become too dangerous. Team sports are only for those who are tough enough physically and socially. The others are encouraged to sit in the bleachers. Skiing on weekends is too expensive for most families. But everybody watches TV or videos or plays computer games, while becoming physically less active.

Canadians and Americans are less fit today than they were ten years ago. Obesity has increased noticeably, even among schoolchildren. Environmentalists tell us that we are now rapidly polluting our air, water, and soil, to the detriment of everyone's health. Children (and adults) are drifting into passive habits of watching and listening, instead of taking an active part in sports, music, drama, and thoughtful discussions. Habitually, they spend hours at a time on TV, computer games, or the phone, while chewing on some well-advertised fast food. They are becoming soft, heavy, and less healthy—more prone to accidents and disease.

A child who is unhealthy either physically *or* emotionally is not likely to show regularity in work done at home or at school. A child who suffers one or more of the following conditions is likely to be sick or absent from school irregularly and often:

- susceptibility to colds, flu, aches, and stomach upsets
- overweight
- poverty
- being from a well-to-do but unregulated home
- feeling unsafe or unwanted at school
- being very shy or withdrawn

Children with these difficulties, especially, require extra attention from parents and teachers if they are to develop reasonably well, and this extra attention costs more in time, work, and money. Because of irregular attendance and uneven effort, these children are also taking up more of the teacher's attention, while showing less progress than their healthy selves would be capable of. The present school system is too costly because it is much too inefficient. Poor health habits are highly uneconomic.

Nutritionists are now calling the public's attention to this serious problem. They are noticing that American and Canadian children have available to them a variety of tempting, sugary soft drinks, which they are in the habit of having between meals. For lunch, they have fat-rich fast foods, like potato chips, with their drinks. Junk foods are conveniently available near schools or *even in schools*. Despite the fact that we are abundantly aware that the health and fitness of our children should be a very important concern, such programs are mostly missing from our regular public school curriculum and cafeterias.

I have seen numerous examples of the lack of seriousness given to health and fitness in the schools over the years. One may be the PE teacher who would stand at the edge of the field yelling at the kids to run faster, while his own belly bulged through his shirt and he munched on his Oh Henry! bar.

We, the voters, are responsible for ignoring this very serious problem. We need to see that the children in our country are not exposed to health-destroying snacks. Children are legally banned from using alcohol and nicotine. Since sugary and fatty foods are also bad for children's health, why not put these harmful substances on the banned list, too?

The growing obesity in school children should tell us that our public school education needs to include a health program that teaches our children the theory and practice of staying healthy. The problem is that schools of today are already expected to do so much more than teaching the basics. Hence, there is little time to include subjects like health, nutrition, and physical fitness. As such, we need a longer school day that includes time to run the necessary, effective health programs for growing children. Not having a comprehensive health and fitness program in grades K through twelve is a serious mistake. Additionally, nonnutritious food should not be available to children. All children who regularly drink soda pop and eat junk food are eating this *instead* of a health-building diet. One way of solving these problems is through the 2SS, where children and staff can choose from a variety of good-tasting, fresh, healthful foods, which are included in the school budget, from the school cafeteria. For the afternoons, the 2SS would have physically active, hands-on programs that would include physical fitness, games for all levels of ability, a choice of sports, community service, and many other projects. Schools in the 2SS would have the time, the buildings, and competent adults in charge. They would also include health as a subject of study, so students can learn and understand how the body functions and what it needs to do so properly.

Unwanted pregnancy and sexually transmitted diseases are other major health-related problems today's young people are facing. I think it is well understood at this point that promiscuity is often one of the results of former child abuse. The 2SS, by supporting children in a big way as they develop, should offset much of this behavior.

There are many methods of protection against pregnancy. However, protections are often not available when needed, especially to young, lower-income women. It is mostly the poor and disadvantaged young women who get caught with the problem of an unwanted pregnancy. Good education and equal, compassionate treatment for all children—hallmarks of the 2SS—would be the best way of trying to eliminate this very big problem for the disadvantaged women in our "democratic" country.

We must make health an important part of everyone's education, training, and responsibility. Young people need the theory (studies in nutrition and physiology), the practice (health and fitness activity program in PE), and a plan to regularly practice proper nutrition (as in the school cafeteria that serves healthful food and drink and nothing else). The idea is to steer children into habits of good nutritional behavior *before* they have a chance to establish health-destroying habits and tastes. The 2SS, with its more concentrated attention on individuals and their unique needs, is a good possibility for remedying this problem.

Promoting Equal Opportunity

Each kind of political-economic system educates its children to support and to sustain its organization and distribution of power. Each system tends to favor the children of those who hold power and has ways of denying an equal chance to be educated to the rest of its subjects. As we have seen lately in newscasts, in Middle Eastern countries, girls are very restricted in what they may do or learn. An obvious imbalance exists in our own country—the gap between rich and poor is growing, as the middle class seems to be shrinking. This imbalance is reflected in our public and private schools. As things are now, it is more difficult for a child from a poor family to get a good education in any school—whether public or private. This is an unfair imbalance of opportunity.

America is splitting into two groups—the minority, who have four-year college educations and draw a comfortable salary, and the majority, who don't and can't keep up with inflation. But in a democratic country, all children have the right to an equal opportunity to get a quality education. Right now, far too many children are out of luck.

The 2SS recognizes this problem to be common in the United States, Canada, and other English-speaking countries as well. Public school education has been losing ground in the past twenty or so years. The No Child Left Behind Act of 2001 increased pressure on schools without providing the necessary improvements to the learning conditions in the United States, and this and similar policies are failing to help children. The two-school system is a plan to put equal opportunity into our schools.

In the 2SS, academic education is for all children. Educators would make great effort toward helping *all* students master *all* the basic concepts in each of the academic courses (language communication, math, science, geography, and history). Children who need more instruction, especially in English, would be given extra individual help during library time in the afternoon.

All children need the basic academic courses to help them understand their future line of work, the political problems they will encounter, and the enjoyment of social life more fully. High school graduation is important to all young people's futures. Separate classes of greater or lesser abilities are, in too many situations, not as productive as are unselected classes that include a variety of talents and abilities. The interaction within heterogeneous classes is conducive to the development of a well-balanced personality, for all students, whether they are very advanced or not. This huge advantage is found only in smaller classes.

The occasional student will work diligently to complete his or her studies but find serious barriers. For example, a grade nine student who I taught found the work difficult. She decided to take two years for each grade thereafter, worked very hard, and completed grade twelve with good marks. She enjoyed a great sense of pride in her accomplishment, and so did her parents and all her teachers.

A few years later, another student, who was in grade eight, asked not to be promoted in June, saying she was not prepared for grade nine and that, in several previous years, she had been pushed on even though she was unready. The counselor told her, "I respect your choice and judgment, but if we held you back, we'd have to hold at least half the class. We would not be allowed to do that." With her parents' support, the student moved to another school, where I hope she was able to progress successfully. Problems like these, wherein students don't have the opportunity to work at the appropriate level should not arise with the 2SS, as child development takes priority over grade levels.

You might say that all students are disabled in different ways and to varying degrees. Everyone needs to learn to respect people of different abilities. And everyone should be respected for who he or she is or for what he or she tries to do well. The 2SS would accommodate special-needs students without having to take time and attention away from other children. Any child who is able to learn the regular school courses should be included in the system, even when special considerations are required. The presence of disabled students in the 2SS would help to enrich the education of *all* the students. Understanding people with different needs is an integral part of this world. Cooperation with, support for, and appreciation of people with different abilities would contribute to all students' education.

If you believe that the poor deserve to be poor, then the two-school system will not be to your liking. The democratic philosophy of education is that every child deserves to be taught at his or her level of understanding— wherever that is. Children may not be excluded from school because they cannot speak English or because they are too hungry or too embarrassed to be able to concentrate on lessons. Additionally, the 2SS would have a cafeteria funded in the school budget, where everybody, including the school staff and the children of families from all income levels, would eat only healthful foods every school day. This is only part of the solution to giving the disadvantaged a better chance, but it is a very important part. Providing equal opportunity for a quality education for children of low-income families is fundamental to democracy.

Eliminating Bullying

Bullying takes myriad forms, and it isn't always so obvious. Let us first look at three examples:

1. Three thirteen year old girls, who we'll call Jennifer, Sarah, and Tiffany, are in the same school. Jennifer has a hard time keeping friends. She is envious of the close friendship between Sarah and Tiffany. In order to drive a wedge in that friendship, Jennifer fabricates a plausible story that features Tiffany saying nasty things about Sarah to other friends. Jennifer confidentially reveals this "information" to Sarah, who is shocked and believes it all. Now Sarah is Jennifer's friend and shuns Tiffany. Tiffany feels isolated and hates both Jennifer and Sarah.

2. Matt is a nine-year-old immigrant who is being teased and shunned because of his accent, his "funny" clothes, and his bewildered look. The children's behavior is excused as "just having fun." However, Matt hates his tormentors more each day, and for him, school is not a happy place.

3. Gerald, sixteen, used to enjoy basketball, but he has been sick with the flu off and on. Now that he's back, the boys don't want him on the team. They express their rejection of him in various verbal and physical ways that hurt his self-esteem. At first he is very depressed. Later his anger turns to a simmering hate, which slowly grows more intense; his studies suffer as well. His teachers are disappointed in him, and he feels neglected and betrayed.

Cool School

In each of the above cases, the negative feeling in the child was destroying what might otherwise have been a positive learning experience. In each case, an initial negative feeling had a way of persisting and becoming a deeper feeling of hatred. The potential for worse to happen was definitely there.

When people (or animals) are free to interact regularly in their groups, an order of power, a pecking order, develops naturally. We see it among wolves, in the chicken yard, and in school yards where supervision is minimal. Among the student population, there is a well-understood pecking order—as there is among less intelligent animals—wherever young people are not under close supervision. Unnoticed by very busy, conscientious teachers, the competition for prestige and for power demands a great deal of attention and energy from each student, no matter where he or she happens to be in the pecking order. For the most part, this activity has a negative influence on positive child development.

The problem is that parents and teachers are aware of what children *should* be doing, thinking, and feeling, but they are not clear on just *what* is preventing students from working and playing with a more positive attitude. What's preventing them is that they are always looking for a comfortable place in the pecking order (which keeps changing, like everything else).

Like cooperation, competition in the pecking order manifests itself in different ways. Some manifestations are rather obvious in their outward appearance. But there is much more to the pecking order among children that is carefully kept below the notice of caring adults. Some examples that are obvious to children but could very well escape the notice of overworked teachers include the following:

1. The pecking order itself
2. Overt snubbing
3. Quiet name-calling
4. Hiding the victim's belongings
5. Unwanted gestures like "the finger"
6. Crude noises to put a victim down
7. Confidential lies about the victim
8. Planned fights and other unfriendly encounters
9. Quiet support for the victimization of a student.

Competition is natural among people and among other living beings. The "bully" system, however, develops naturally in recurring situations where children are not properly supervised. It is so common that it seems that every schoolboy and girl is well aware of it. It seems that every student knows his or her position in the bullying system of the local area. The positions usually include one top bully; a few close supporters; a large number of spectators who "do nothing" but are, by their presence, necessary supporters; and the victim(s), usually just one child at a time and sometimes as a very small group. A bully is a successful competitor who has gained prestige and power; he or she is usually not really "worse" than anyone else, just more influential.

The problem with bullying is that this kind of recreation, which involves hurting certain weaker individuals repeatedly over time, is very harmful.

It is harmful to:

a) the victims
b) the bully's followers (who see the bully as a role model)
c) the bully
d) the cause of education in that community
e) our youngsters' understanding of what democracy requires.

In the adult world, the "bully system" manifests in situations where the strongest, meanest, nastiest competitor takes all, in the mostly unregulated "free" world of theirs. This is no place for people who believe in fairness or in striving for a democratic way of life. At its essence, bullying is a form of unfair competition.

Although bullies may be natural, they are also *unnecessary*. To schools, they are counterproductive. Generally speaking, students who are independent and unaffected by the system have well-developed personalities and have had the benefit of much consistent support and training. They have strong adult backup. Well-ordered schools channel competitive energy from where it would be destructive to learning to where it is used to improve students' efforts to learn more efficiently. A healthy community keeps would-be bullies preoccupied. This requires intelligent supervision with some control. In the 2SS children would work on activities that are suited to their abilities and their interests, giving them a reasonably competitive chance with those of a similar ability level. In that way, much of the activity takes on the form of cooperation, as well as of some friendly competition. The longer school day prevents the nasty and unfair variety of competition from developing, which usually happens when children are unsupervised and unguided. Instead of making "bullies," this system would develop experts, who could lead in their own special strengths—be those in athletics, debating, music, drama, mathematics, writing, computers, or any other arena. Instead of having to become a bully to obtain power and prestige, a student would want to excel in an activity that was of special interest to him or her. Being relieved from former harassment, the student would happily become involved in educational activities.

Late recognition of the problem of bullying has become a concern for most educators. When teachers realize that their workload does not allow them to correct the situation, they are forced to try not to notice the problems that are beyond their reach. Teachers of large classes are also likely to miss the subtle bullying in school time, which is often more destructive than the overt kind. Again, the 2SS will be well prepared to identify and manage such issues early on because of its small class sizes.

Despite being minimized, bullying may very well surface now and then, even in the 2SS. The question, then, is how the 2SS would handle such situations—both their short-term effects and their long-term effects. Zero-tolerance is a common answer, but I propose that it isn't a true solution.

Zero-tolerance means that, if you cross a certain line designated by the powers that be, you have gone too far, and you automatically get a penalty.

On the surface, it seems fair enough. And this policy does make functioning in the short-term easier for the school, but it does not correct the underlying cause. *Expelling a student means that the school system failed* to develop this young person educationally and emotionally. The student did not get the education that he or she needed. He or she was probably handed a very poor start in life, and expulsion did not solve the problem. In short, zero-tolerance is a neat, straightforward, *temporary* solution to a very vexing problem. It is not a way of solving it, but rather a way of pushing it away for someone else to deal with. It is another way of telling problem people that they are unimportant.

Most of us know of some cases where a child is subtly bullied on the school bus, around school, and during school time. Subtle bullying is more damaging to one's self-respect than the overt kind, because, when the victim complains to parents, bus drivers, or teachers, the complaint is often not taken seriously. What if these people lose their *patience*, though? What if they have learned, from our acts of zero-tolerance with them, to have zero-tolerance when dealing with those who oppress them?

On a global scale, we are afraid of impatient, angry, marginalized people. There are very many of them today, and a good number of them could easily be "terrorists." Should they be jailed or more efficiently killed? How would you know that you are killing the right people? Marginalized people are likely to be resentful. As children who are marginalized get older, they often seek ways to combat years of feeling depressed, unseen, and unable to defend themselves and start asking, "How do I get even with the people who have been putting me down?" People who think that zero-tolerance is the right solution are only painting themselves and society into a corner. Our present impersonal, large school system is, for the most part, to blame. We need to try the kinder, friendlier, more interesting 2SS to help us develop a generation that thinks and feels more positively to help improve the lifestyles and attitudes of the people of the future.

The 2SS seems to be the best way to avoid marginalizing people. In this system, primary classes are limited to twelve (or fewer) students per teacher. The low pupil to teacher ratio facilitates communication between the teacher and individual children. Under these conditions, children can build a very desirable foundation of positive attitudes, good work habits, many social skills, and a healthy self-confidence. No one is marginalized in the 2SS. What about zero-tolerance? This situation could not develop in the 2SS.

The parents of normally progressing, well-behaved children may wonder why they should be concerned about other people's children, who have for some reason been neglected and are now having difficulties. The response is simple; these students who have problems affect the learning environment of all the other pupils. Parents in the community must observe not only what kind of teacher their child has but also what kind of students are in the class. With a little extra help given early, most students become encouraged and do much better. Seeing how those students with deficiencies can actually overcome them has a good effect on the better students. There is a direct beneficial effect on the stronger students, because the learning atmosphere remains positive. This strategy is most effective in small classes.

Advantages for Parents

The 2SS would take a great amount of strain off of parents, but it will not and cannot replace them. It will, however, give them the effective help that they must have these days.

For one, parents would have fewer problems to deal with at home, because children would be purposefully occupied and steadily developing positive habits and attitudes until 5:00 p.m. Adults could enjoy seeing how well their children are developing into pleasant, capable people. Parents would become happier and less tired. With the dependable time structure of the 2SS, there would be better communication between children and parents and between parents and teachers. Following are some other opportunities created by the 2SS:

- On a school day, parents and children would leave the house at about the same time, before 8:00 a.m. Thus, use of bathroom and kitchen would need to be organized—a good opportunity to practice cooperation and consideration.

- In many homes, children and parents would arrive home around the same time, soon after 5:00 p.m. Life around home would become more predictable, more positive, and therefore, more manageable for parents. Also, everybody could help with preparing, serving, and cleaning up from supper. Parents would be there to guide the children. This could facilitate fairness in doing of chores. Parents and children would become more connected. This is so important to the success and happiness of the family.

- Parents could rest assured that their children are spending their precious weekdays learning what they need in order to achieve a long and happy life. Although parents have the greatest interest in the health and education of their children, they lose much of their influence and control to larger factors in the community. They cannot do much about the forces that would encourage their children to eat junk food; try drugs; avoid doing homework; pressure them to buy expensive, unnecessary items; and engage in unsanitary or otherwise dangerous activities. The structured, longer school day would keep these children safe from destructive behaviors.

- Children would be healthier and become more interested in school, resulting in fewer sick days and missed lessons.

Children's sick days not only interrupt the flow of their lessons, but it also can mean that a parent has to take time off paying work to stay home with the child or hire a sitter. Either way, this eats into the household budget, negatively affects parent job demands, and generally elevates stress in the home.

- Children would have had so much time with their classmates that they would be ready for the change of just being at home with their approving parents outside of school time. All members of the family could become more involved with and supportive of each other.

- Parents would be very happy to notice that their children were becoming well educated in core subjects, as well as in the skills and knowledge related to positive learning. This promises to be a very good way for parents to reconnect with their children!

- As teachers would be less overstressed, they would take fewer days of sick leave, which would mean fewer school days managed by substitute teachers. Less stress to the child should mean less worry for the parent.

- Better continuity in the learning patterns of their children would make for much better results. Assurance that the child is learning alleviates concern in the parent.

- Parents will have the pleasure of noticing that, when all children look forward to going to school every day, their reduced free time actually reinforces their enthusiasm for learning.

- With improved accomplishment and less stress during the weekdays, the weekends have a good chance of becoming enjoyable family time.

- Only teachers with the ability to keep children involved and interested would continue to keep their positions in the school. It would be easy to replace them because of the good learning conditions. Assurance that their child is well served educationally alleviates parental worries.

Despite all these benefits of the 2SS, it's important to note that the love, security, moral guidance, and privacy that a child should get at home can be achieved only within the protective family. Community institutions, like churches and schools, however, can support and reinforce the influence and training a child gets at home. A school can try to give the child the same things that a good parent does but in a more public way. The 2SS builds on what parents do well.

Blaming parents for what their young people do gets us nowhere. Parents have to work too hard for a living to be able to do the whole, very difficult job of guiding and influencing their children. Parents do not have the money, the energy, or the time to do it all. Nor should they need to.

Because most families today need both parents to work in order to have enough money to raise their children, parents cannot be with their children after school and on weekends—the very times when they would like to be training, influencing, and guiding their children. Although parents try very hard, effective child rearing is not possible for most of them. Parents who are unemployed may have more time to study their children's difficulties, but because of a severe shortage of money, they may be frustrated and unable to help their children. Despondency in parents is not conducive to desirable child development. Frequent scolding or other punishment (often the result of stress) will not result in the desired child development.

Estimated Average Cost of Raising Two Children
(Born two years apart) circa 1990 Canada until HS graduation:

Expense	Dollars	Time in a Year		Number of Years or Commitment		Annual Cost
Rent	$100	x 12 months	x	20	=	$ 24,000
Food	30	x 365 days	x	20	=	219,000
Clothing	100	x 12 months	x	20	=	24,000
Transportation	20	x 12 months	x	20	=	4,800
Gifts	20	x 12 months	x	20	=	4,800
Emergencies	15	x 12 months	x	20	=	3,600
Total						**$280,200**

The most invisible cost of raising children is the unpaid mother's work with the father's help:

$10 x 10 hours x 365 days x 20 years = $730,000

Parents do have a responsibility and most of them are trying very hard to meet that responsibility, but so do other adults have a responsibility here, which they are *not* recognizing. Society needs to recognize that parenting is, directly or indirectly, extremely important to *everyone's* welfare, *and* that parenting requires, on average, at least as much time, energy, and know-how as most careers do. In a democratic society, the work of raising the next generation must always be a constructive community effort. If we put the full burden of raising children of each family on that family's parents, as we can see, society will destroy itself. Parents cannot and should not be expected to do what is not possible. Without community support, they cannot do a satisfactory job of raising children. The proposed 2SS is a plan to ensure that our public schools do what the community and the extended family used to but can no longer do to help raise children who later become good, solid citizens.

Unfortunately, in the present free market economy, we neglect to count the cost of producing male and female workers. Traditionally, mothers did virtually all of the nurturing and training of children until children had reached a teenage level of strength, skill, and self-confidence. (Fathers used to take over the guidance of their sons at about age twelve into the accepted ways of men. Because of the rising cost of living, modern technology, and unpaid and unrecognized work done in the home, in addition to the widening gap between the rich and the poor and the shrinking middle class, it is common now for a woman to work at two jobs—her unpaid job at home and her career, from which she achieves social recognition and a wage or salary to augment the family income.

Without the nurturing, training, and guidance that children used to get from Mother (with some help from Father), many of our legally adult children are *not ready* to leave home and enter the "real world" as well-trained, well-educated, well-spoken, strong and healthy, responsible young adults. Instead, too many of them remain financially dependent on parents and unemployable for various understandable reasons. The 2SS is well poised to relieve parents of these outcomes.

Advantages for Teachers

It follows that, if children and parents are happy and enthusiastic, teachers are more likely to be happy and enthusiastic as well. They can do the jobs they intended to do when they chose their career path. The 2SS would give them many advantages, including the following:

- The work of teaching and managing children would be less stressful and much more productive. Teachers would have ample time and space to prepare lessons and to mark student assignments more promptly, as there would be a set of teachers for the morning instruction and another staff for the afternoon lessons. The teachers would have either the afternoon or the morning for their lesson preparation and marking, depending on which shift they taught. This would allow teaching staff to have evenings free to concentrate on their own families at home.

- Better rested and better prepared teachers would result in more effective lessons.
- Schools with fewer disruptions would have fewer learning and discipline problems.
- Our good teachers would not be as tempted as they are now to change careers.
- Every child would want to be at school on a school day because of the enjoyable learning conditions.

"Overtime"...

Teachers of large classes and at large schools cannot be very effective, particularly because they are busy managing behavior when they should be able to teach lessons, as discussed throughout this book. To me, the large public school is looking more and more like a holding place for children until they become old enough to be employed in places where obedience and compliance, plus a few skills, are required. Good learning conditions have been deteriorating and are being "corrected" with government-imposed standardized testing. We are only *beginning* to feel the results of this shift away from seriously providing a good education for all of our children. Competent teachers feel this deterioration and see that many of their serious efforts are no longer very effective, when their own governments no longer seem interested in seeing to the real needs of a public school.

Teachers, in general, feel very strongly that every child has the right to a high-quality education and a good upbringing. They are very happy when conditions for learning are favorable and when children come to school eager to learn. Good teachers love to teach all schoolchildren—the weak and the strong. However, both students and teachers become frustrated and discouraged when poor learning conditions continue to worsen through government cutbacks or larger classes.

The 2SS aims to provide working conditions that are right for continued success. This system will attract and develop the most dedicated teachers, especially the many excellent ones who left because they rejected the poor working conditions in the classrooms. The 2SS is a plan that puts children's needs first, thus solving most of our other problems.

Advantages for School Administration

Because the children, parents, and teachers would all benefit from the 2SS and experience the joy and satisfaction that result, school administrators would find their work easier and more enjoyable as well. They could focus more on growth than on problem resolution—a win-win for all. More specifically, in the 2SS school boards would find the following:

- It easier to hire good teachers.
- Teacher assistants would be happier because there would be more harmony in the classroom.
- Janitors could have regular work days from 8:00 a.m. to 4:00 p.m., with an hour off for free lunch in the cafeteria, working in the "hands-on" building in the mornings and in the academic building in the afternoons.
- Less damage to school property would occur.
- Fewer, if any, suspensions would be necessary.
- Parents are more satisfied.
- The public would again see teens as good people and graduates as real achievers.

- Fewer sick-teacher days would mean better education and less money spent on substitutes.
- Managing the progress of our children correctly in the first place will make the size and number of expensive problems much smaller, so that taxes could be spent on the more positive aspects of schooling.

Just as for teachers, administrative jobs would become more enjoyable and manageable, and education would be an enjoyable opportunity—as it was meant to be.

Advantages for Society

As you might imagine, the benefits of the 2SS would extend beyond the family and the local schools and school districts to the surrounding communities and the country and world at large. The results of raising healthy, intelligent, and well-adjusted young people would affect greater numbers of people as the graduates moved out into the world and did their work; the benefits of this system would also have a ripple effect, as the graduates influenced their peers (and perhaps even their elders) and as they bore and raised children in the ways that they were raised. The benefits would be manifold, but the greatest advantages pertain to the economy and business, as well as to the environment and our society's overall morale. The following sections highlight some of the most prominent benefits that could be realized through the 2SS.

The Economy

Taxpayers are already paying a huge amount of money to support the public education system. It is obvious that many of the children are not making the best use of their opportunities for an education. Why should we waste even more money on schools? Because if we don't, our problems will only continue to compound.

Let us look at the problem. We are already spending far too much money on dealing with and caring for the various misfits that are coming out of our schools. We are now paying for twenty-five hours of public class-time for students each week which, admittedly, uses up millions of dollars. It turns out that, during the rest of the week, large numbers of schoolchildren are left to their own devices. During this aimless free time, they are busy watching TV, playing computer games, talking to their friends, or hanging around the neighborhood "looking for trouble." These are all excellent ways to cancel from their memories what they learned at school that day. Ensuring that these young people were involved in some sports or doing some guided physical work or other engaging activity would minimize the expenses associated with all this aimless, unprotected, unsupervised time. These problems are mostly long lasting, difficult, and very expensive to correct. Nevertheless, the injured parties, the accused young adults (often the wrong ones, at first), the legal system, the police, the social workers, the jails, the health professionals, the insurance companies, as well as the school teachers, all cost money to the taxpayer, directly or indirectly. By lessening these occurrences through spending more money upfront, we would relieve the taxpayers' burden in the long run.

Simply put, shortsighted thinking is not going to solve the tremendous problems stemming from undisciplined, uneducated, and unguided young people. The results from this heavy expenditure are poor, and these problems are never fully resolved. Too many of these young people will continue to be expensive problems for society for many years to come—a continuing expense for property owners and for our government.

We cannot blame the children for being so misguided; it is our own fault for having overlooked the importance of their needs as children and as students, as well as their importance in our society. To turn this problem around, we need to set our priorities where we think they should be. If we really do love children, then we will put their welfare first. As early as possible (preferably before birth), we must see that children are well cared for, physically and emotionally. And then we could work on providing children with a comprehensive education, one that would prepare them for a happy life of contributing their best to society—thereby building a better life for everyone. At the same time, *taxes could decrease* to noticeably less than what they are now—at least, as far as education expenses and the associated trickle-down costs are concerned.

I estimate that, within a couple of years of working in the two-school system, one should notice a definite improvement in the behavior and personal development of schoolchildren. After five or six years of this kind of schooling, we would begin to see some welcome improvements in our society. In ten years, far fewer misfits would emerge from our secondary schools. The cost of housing and looking after misfits would be greatly reduced. Instead of becoming burdens to taxpayers, these graduates would become great assets to our communities. *Heavy taxation on the general public would no longer be necessary.*

Another economic concern with directing more funding to education is the belief that there are too many people in the world and that the more you help those in need, the more the population increases. It is true that plants and animals tend to multiply when the right amounts of suitable food, water, and air are available. In some cases, they tend to multiply even more when under much stress. However, when human communities become economically comfortable and have more control over their own lives, such as having smaller families, they can afford to spend valuable time and money for their children's development.

Here is an observation from Joanne of Burnaby, BC, who was a teacher and proud mother of two girls.

> When girls are educated, they no longer see child raising as their sole goal. They want a challenging job and life that allows them to express themselves first. Having children is important, but is postponed until their personal development is completed. Once the decision to have a child has been made, they approach it with serious maturity, and the child is the benefactor. Should the marriage or partnership break down, she is in a better position to provide for the child economically and emotionally. Such a parent would more likely support the 2SS and be an active participant in the child's education.

So education for all children equally is key to the very serious problem of overpopulation.

A side benefit to an initial increase in public school funding is the long-term increase in jobs; adults in the community with talents in special fields (like piano, ballet, jazz, tap dancing, gymnastics, voice, coaching a sport, karate, acting, and on and on) could find part-time work in the afternoons at the school—paid by the school board.

All things considered, the two-school system is well within what society can and must afford—never mind what our governments or political leaders tell us. We cannot afford to have the future of our children shortchanged any longer. Nor can our society afford to have so many of our qualified, talented adults unemployed or underpaid when there is so much work of quality needing to be done!

Business

Another aspect of the economy that would change for the better upon adoption of the 2SS is the workforce. Business in general would become stronger because our schools would be graduating more intelligent, capable, and responsible new workers. These workers would be more reliable and more trainable to boot because these virtues will have been instilled in them consistently through their growing years. Young workers would be more motivated and productive through the strong support system at school and reduced stress at home, and more graduates would be interested in further education because they will have grown to love learning.

Side benefits in the workplace would also result from having more well-rounded, healthy adults. These benefits would include

- far less harassment in the workplace;
- less trouble with safety rules;
- reduced loitering;
- less damage to property and less stealing;
- better manners from young people;
- people who grow up not needing to lie and, therefore, more honest workers; and
- more time for medical and social services people to do preventive work, because they will not have to deal with problems arising out of unsupervised activity.

Consider, also, the marketplace. In general, more employed people means more customers.

While this is true, it's also true that the interests of community and those of business are sometimes at odds. For example, let's take the case of the fast food market. Free enterprise is strong on competition, whereas public schools exist to teach intelligent cooperation and healthful living. A student in the 2SS who is taught the theory of health and the practice of fitness would tend to choose his or her snacks more intelligently. When the same student becomes an adult and has children, his or her offspring will have a much better chance than others of being psychologically and physically healthy, thus being a smaller burden on the public health system. This health-conscious adult's family is likely to remain relatively free from the burdens of common health problems that children of today have, such as earaches, obesity, diabetes, leukemia, colds, poor teeth, allergies, or psychological problems that prevent learning. The children would probably grow up to become helpful, responsible members of their communities. Instead of burdens, they would become assets to their communities.

What does this do to the businesses selling products that are harmful to health? I believe the following is likely to occur. With serious health education in our public schools, public demand for products would change slowly, and producers of fast foods would surely adapt without much problem. Successful businesses are always ready to adapt their efforts to suit the changing demands of their paying customers. Fast food outlets would change their products and their advertising to suit the changing demands for more healthful fast foods. For example, the baby carrots and the small cans of V8 juice currently available in most grocery stores are fairly new and very successful fast foods because people are becoming more health conscious. So, yes, the 2SS would graduate more intelligent consumers—and most businesses would adapt to the changing market. A few others would, at first, resist, but to stay in business, they would adjust to market demands and the 2SS in a matter of time.

The Environment

Environmental problems close to home, as well as globally, are becoming more serious from year to year. Let's look at a few, as well as the solutions that the 2SS could help us to work toward:

- These days, litter is left behind wherever children and adults spend their free, unsupervised time. Everyone could do with some training in orderliness and responsibility and the development of positive peer pressure that would occur in the 2SS.
- Chemicals contaminate our foods, toys, cosmetics, building materials, air, and water, to name a few. Practical science courses could go a long way toward preventing future health problems caused today by mysterious chemical poisons in our living space. The 2SS would be committed to incorporating science as it affects a child's daily living.

Society's Overall Morale

In addition to the sense of security that comes with more stable businesses (and, in turn, a more stable economy), as well as the pride that comes with taking care of our environment, the 2SS would yield side benefits to society's overall morale. Fewer business owners and citizens would need to be concerned with public disturbances.

In particular, we could look forward to the following results:

- We would have fewer teens with "problems," wandering around, looking for vulnerable people or unprotected property. As such, there would be fewer car thefts and less damage to buildings.

- Noise disturbances would be lessened, and productivity, as well as true relaxation, would be enhanced, as young people would be trained to practice self-control. Some of our young people (and their parents) are not aware that the noise level in homes, schools, workplaces, and public spaces is often too great for the good of the people there. The noise for some people is so pervasive that it prevents them from thinking clearly, causing poor judgment and unnecessary stress—all of which can lead to hearing loss and serious accidents, as well as less good work being done each day. The 2SS fosters community-mindedness as well as respect for self and for others.

- There would be less graffiti on business places, less stealing in shops, and better communication between teenagers and business people. This improved connection between business people and teenagers could translate into more businesses wanting to hire teenagers to help in their operations.

- Our young people would become more civilized, more likeable, and more welcome in adult company. These responsible young people would be *welcomed* into many adult organizations representing a great number of interests. Adults would become less critical of children. Overall, a more positive atmosphere would prevail.

Keep in mind that these are only some of the benefits that could be realized as a result of this new school system, and they are promising and make it worth trying. Other benefits could emerge over time after the plan is implemented and as it evolves. This brings us to the next point of discussion. How might we even begin making such major changes in our education system? The next chapter provides food for thought (and action, of course).

Chapter 4

How We Can Make It Happen

THERE ARE THREE DEFINITE ways to live one's formative years—constructively, passively, and destructively. These lifestyles pertain to the individual as well as to our decisions as a society. Because this is the chapter where I encourage you to start thinking about how to implement the 2SS in your own area, this is also a good place to consider your options overall. Please consider the following:

1. The *constructive or positive life* consists of learning how to make things better for every individual in the community. We have the builders and supporters of our present level of democracy to thank for our many freedoms in the forms of our roads, hospitals, public schools, freedom of religion, and democratic government.

2. The *passive or do-nothing life* consists of watching TV and playing computer games and of becoming ever more skilled at avoiding responsibility and work. Young people who are lazy, in time, easily become perpetual dependents.

3. The *destructive life* consists of bullying, quarreling, fighting, smoking, overeating, all of which cause huge costs in time, money, and materials and unhappiness in people's lives.

In our present democracy, it is still possible for us to choose the constructive form of government, which is able to view children as more than just future workers to help companies make profits. Our children are ourselves in the future. The new world is what we make it. Some of us have been watching TV too much and believe that we can have no say in what is happening globally or in what is happening with our children. Everything is controlled by the bottom line. Or is it? Are our children really for sale?

In a democracy, if the citizens are educated to think for themselves, the voters can give valuable support and direction to public school policy. The reader of this book *can* make a positive or negative difference. This chapter helps you get started.

Managing Finances: Up-Front Costs, Long-Term Savings

In the short term, the cost of education looks very expensive. Making important changes always costs money to begin with. School buildings, equipment, and personnel together cost millions, with almost no *immediate* return for this very big investment. To begin with, a community would be spending at least twice as much on public education per year. You would need more classroom space and twice as many teachers or leaders with the right qualifications. The best perspective, however, is one that sees education as a long-term investment, one that *yields extremely profitable returns for society* in general. There would be many substantial economic gains to be made in addition to the social, political, and national benefits. In order to see these gains, many of us may need to redefine our understanding of success.

Many people measure success in dollars. At the American and Canadian national level, in fact, the gross domestic product is measured in dollars and includes only that which can be conveniently measured in dollars (such as raw materials, manufactured goods, salaries, and wages). This is an easy but misleading way of measuring our nation's success. Not included in our figuring are these important factors:

- the deterioration of the environment
- the loss of children's chances of growing up educated and healthy
- the work done by volunteers, homemakers, and other caregivers

Cool School

The overemphasis on short-term, bottom-line figures is underserving our future. We need, instead, to move in a direction that looks toward investing in long-term growth and sustainability, as we develop the 2SS. The 2SS would begin to work toward a more balanced measure in terms of how we prepare our children for a better life and would measure success through reduced crime rates, a more efficient, more motivated workforce, and other nonmonetary but equally important measures.

Investment, of course, would be substantial up front but would be increasingly worth it over the long term. If funding is the greatest concern for you, consider how much we are currently wasting as a result of inefficient policies in public education. These days, we are needlessly spending money dealing with and caring for the various misfits that are coming out of today's inefficient schools. At present, we are foolishly "saving money" through cutbacks in education and reduced spending on the very necessary needs of our young people. When we change from small schools to large, consolidated schools served by school buses for ten or more kilometers around, we think we save some tax money, but the quality of education that children receive is very much reduced.

As everybody knows, with the present system of educating children, the long-term bad results become *very* costly for a very long time. Some of these costly results are

- our very polluted environment, which is quickly becoming more so; and
- continued lack of leadership for our youth, which easily leads to break-ins, accidents, shoplifting, shootings, suicides, fires, car thefts, harassment, and rape.

The above problems lead to another set of expenses, among them, medical and legal costs and those associated with law enforcement, imprisonment, insurance, and social service. These expenses are the results of former shortsighted government planning. Purely political decisions look to the short term (usually less than four years into the future). Short-term planning for child development is, as a rule, extremely uneconomic.

Our young people are not equipped to avoid the above problems. Therefore, the problems cost taxpayers. To turn this problem around, we need to set our priorities where we think they *should* be.

In particular, we need more taxes coming from the corporations who profit from effective public school education. Since converting to the 2SS would benefit businesses directly—providing them with a more capable, more dependable, and more adaptable workforce and, therefore, more profits, in addition to a larger paying customer base in the future—one might expect businesses to willingly support this change. Despite this simple logic, though, convincing some organizations will be like pulling teeth.

However, I believe the social climate is changing. Recently, in October 2011, public protests have been brewing into a massive movement, starting on Wall Street in New York and spreading across the United States, over to Europe, and into Canada. These protestors largely are expressing their urgent and overdue need to be kept in the fair equation of prosperity, as corporations grow more wealthy and powerful. They are mothers, fathers, grandparents; workers, business owners, and the underemployed—all kinds of people. They claim to be the 90+ percent of people who need to be heard! We cannot know at this point what the outcome will be, *but* the way in which a movement can grow when people truly know what they stand for is not insignificant. This historical event shows how people who care can be noticed and heard! I do not advocate anything like insurgence, but in a true democracy, everyone's voice should have some say, and children need their adults to speak up for them.

Just how much is a child's future worth? If we continue to "save money on public education," what are the long-term disasters awaiting our beloved children in the years to come? They are many, including

- unnecessary poor achievement for many children in our schools;
- abuse of alcohol, tobacco, drugs, and even medications;
- precious developmental time and money wasted on expensive clothes, computer games, and other toys with very little in the way of good long-term results; and
- huge new medical problems that stem from the very noticeable increase in the rate of teen pregnancies and future diseases caused by present obesity.

It is up to people like you and me to do all we can now to avoid this hellish future awaiting today's families. As I've explained in previous chapters, the 2SS is a logical solution. Once established, it would be **very** economical.

After the first year, the cost would become progressively less until it reaches a very comfortable, workable level. It would be *more economical* because of its positive effectiveness and because of its easy elimination of the sources of our most serious problems in terms of raising and educating the youth today. This investment would bring down our present huge costs in law enforcement, legal expenses, prisons, health care, insurance, welfare, damage control, and public relations. For example, less frustration and more time and energy for outdoor recreation would also result in better health for children, teachers, and parents, leading to fewer medical expenses and more good work accomplished. As soon as a year later this investment would begin to yield dividends in the form of a more controlled, happier life for people in every socioeconomic level, as well as saving money for the taxpayers.

Much improved public school education would also cancel a large part of the cost of previous problems resulting from today's public and private child neglect. The overall change would be, in a few years, more safety and more happiness for all citizens. We might be pleasantly surprised with the noticeable improvement in learning.

More people would be employed, thereby improving the strength in the economy and increasing the well-being of more citizens. The workday could be reduced to about seven or six hours, making for less-tired parents and less unemployment. Teachers, parents, police, medical caregivers, and social workers would be faced with *reasonable* workloads. Teaching would become a very desirable profession again, attracting more good people.

Most parents would also begin to notice welcome changes in their children's attitudes toward school very early in the fall. Within a couple of years of working with the two-school system, the public would notice a definite improvement in the behavior of schoolchildren. It would give conscientious parents a much better chance to bring their children up the way they wish. It would save much of the time and money that they spend on expensive "reward" items that don't work very well anyway. Parents with no parental experience would be able to do a successful job with their children because their offspring would be picking up more good habits and experiences and fewer destructive ones as the school days pass. With the 2SS, children with weak parental support would stand a *much better* chance to prepare themselves for adulthood for the same reasons. After five or six years of this kind of schooling, the big improvements would begin to really show; self-confident graduates with great hopes for a positive future would emerge from our secondary schools.

In twelve years, the transformation in our society would be *nearly* complete. Graduates emerging from the 2SS would be trained and educated to become valuable, self-respecting workers and responsible, caring, intelligent citizens who want to do what is best for all concerned, knowing that recognition and appreciation for their efforts will usually be forthcoming.

If we really do love children or if we realize that they are our future, then we will put their welfare first. And then we could work on providing them with a comprehensive education—one that would prepare them for a happy life of contributing their best efforts to society and of building a better way of life in the community for all ages (instead of destroying it).

At present, we are doing less than a half job of schooling and of raising our children. We need to see that what the school teaches in the morning does not get cancelled by negative influences in the afternoon and evening. For proper development, it is very important that children are happy but suitably challenged most of the day—be it at work or at play. It is time we try the 2SS. It stands to reason that *effective public school education would cost less* in the long run and the benefits would continue for generations to come.

Today, the public schools (underfunded and overloaded as they have become) are still the best hope we have if we wish to continue living in a caring, equitable society that is inclusive. But improve them we must!

In order to achieve a very favorable learning environment for our children, public schools would need to be financed through public revenue from taxes. If rich countries like Canada and the United States cannot afford to raise enough taxes to pay for a pollution-free public school, then we really do have our priorities wrong.

Order of Operations

I can't give you a tried-and-true method for getting the 2SS up and running in your area because so many factors are part of that decision process, but I can give you some general guidelines for how the process should flow:

1. Everything starts with the parent who understands the need. These ideas must then be shared and developed with a few more local parents.
   a) Read *Cool School* and study the parts that interest you the most.
   b) Find two or three other parents who agree with you.

c) Discuss the ideas in *Cool School* and how these changes would affect children you know well and others.

d) Talk about the possibilities of having a small pilot school in one of the larger buildings nearby, that get used only on weekends—a hall or a church.

2. The next step could be to have informal meetings that include some interested teachers, who may wish later to include their principal. These meetings initially could be to brainstorm the possibilities.

3. The group (parents, teachers, principal, board members, and/or others who have some good ideas) has meetings to discuss the matter further. The first objective of this larger group of leaders would be to establish a pilot project in inexpensive but promising locations, like empty buildings and public recreational areas. We would need to encourage talented community members to assist the superintendent in planning and preparing to try the 2SS to see what it takes and how it can make a difference. A small group of parents and teachers in the community (four or more) would meet to discuss suggestions as to where to begin to effect changes for improvement in our school system. Everybody in your group would have suggestions and questions. There could be a number of notable changes emphasizing:

- Serious consideration for each and every student according to his or her needs
- Noticeably better recognition for primary students and their teachers and for their importance in the system – This section of the school has, in the past, not been able to demand and get its share of the funding per child.
- Greater emphasis on health and fitness at all levels, for all students equally
- *Initial* emphasis on the child's continued interest in a subject rather than on his or her test results – In later grades, emphasis on interested involvement and test results would tend to be equal. (Pressuring children to learn may produce some positive results, but the damage to attitude could also produce *more* problems.)

The success of this pilot school will help to interest families in switching to this new, very popular public school system. I estimate that, after two or three years of pilot projects, a growing number of communities would be ready to embrace the implementation of the 2SS.

Piloting the Program

Schools are institutions that need *time* to earn general acceptance from the people they serve. To establish a new school system like the 2SS would require that we begin with just two or three school districts using existing, available buildings and hiring highly qualified or motivated additional staff. This would give the stakeholders and the public time to study this very successful school and watch it in operation while the professionals worked on the glitches. The next step would be to establish the system in the places where the parents are demanding this change. For administrators, teachers, and school boards, the pilot project would tell them what aspects needed improvement.

Each pilot project would have its own special circumstances and problems. The people on the planning committee would need to represent the wishes of the community, and a democratic government should provide all funding. If the voting public saw the need for better public school education, the politicians in the government would *want* to lead the way to more effective funding for our public schools.

The pilot project for the 2SS would require more leadership for the improvement process that would follow. This leadership could come from forward-looking, responsible members of our community, who have the confidence of parents and teachers.

One of the foremost concerns in implementing the 2SS is hiring competent teachers. This would take two or three years to accomplish, beginning with a pilot project. In time, though, excellent teachers would be drawn to this school; good learning conditions are very important to excellent teachers. In order to entice strong teachers and keep them in the profession during this time of trial, so to speak, consider the following guidance:

- In advertising a teaching position, a reasonable salary with superior working conditions will attract suitable applicants, as well as others.

- A clear philosophy of education for the school will provide the necessary direction for teachers to plan their lessons.
- Once you have a good staff, you need adequate accommodation for the learning process to take place. Otherwise, some of our best, most dedicated teachers soon will be looking elsewhere to teach. This includes a suitable classroom with supplies available.
- Class size affects the quality of learning, which strongly affects the teacher's satisfaction with the position. Unreasonable class size *does* influence a good teacher to go into some other profession.
- Freedom to teach in the ways that work best for each particular class and for each teacher is important. It allows the teacher to use his or her talents best and to meet the specific needs of a class. Additionally, bear in mind that there is little use in hiring very good teachers unless they have more say in how the money for education is going to be spent. If teachers and principals are in control of the resources, they can, in a systematic way, use the money where it will do the most good. Good teachers *need* flexibility. They should be consulted when new school buildings are being planned.
- Ensure that teachers have enough time for lesson preparation, marking, professional development, staff meetings, and meetings with parents
- Regular times and places for teachers to compare notes and to develop fresh ideas are imperative.
- Office and library support allow teachers to do their best work.
- Ensure that teachers and students are recognized for what they do well; recognition can be informal or otherwise. Positive reinforcement is an effective motivator.

If we can show that we are serious about putting children first, we will, at the same time, attract and keep the best teachers. Good teachers put children first.

Some parents may be worried about teachers who are in the system only to collect salary. Improving learning conditions would definitely encourage good teachers to stay and to do a better job. Actually, if teachers were given good working conditions, *they would realize that parents cared.*

Then most of them would transform into excellent, conscientious teachers, and the rest of the staff members would likewise work at their best. When learning conditions improve, some caring but struggling teachers will not want to leave because they will become more effective teachers under these new conditions and they would be mostly right! Deliberate nonperformers would soon feel very uncomfortable in this constructive environment of 2SS. In a school where everyone's success is appreciated, where one's ideas are welcomed, and where rules are fair, nonperformers would feel quite out of place. Their excuses for nonperformance would be gone. Such people, I am sure, would leave of their own accord.

These same 2SS conditions will attract competent, hardworking candidates, as well as others, for new teaching positions. It will be up to the school board to get all the intelligent help they can before choosing new staff and to have a "temporary contract" to facilitate correcting the occasional wrong choice.

During the first year of operation in an existing school building, this new system would have many glitches that would show up in different places. Most of the many minor problems would be solved then. A successful changeover to the 2SS would depend on intelligent guidance and support from those involved one way or another.

Involved people would include (among others) parents, students, teachers, and support staff. However, we would need one professional educator, with a number of special advisors, to guide the changeover. This job would probably go to the superintendent, if there is one, with the very important help and involvement of the principals, who would communicate with teachers.

Students, parents, and teachers would be encouraged to give feedback to principals, superintendents, and other teachers. All complaints and suggestions would be taken seriously and adjustments considered.

Finding Good Leadership

To change from the present system to the 2SS, we would need principals and superintendents who are leaders, *not dictators*. They would have to be the kind of people who do more listening than talking—people who are short-term planners and long-term thinkers. They will need to do some actual teaching in the classroom and much supervising in the new operation so that they can fine-tune the change while making small improvements and correcting any problems as soon as they appear. The changeover is bound to have some unforeseen glitches that the principal would be in the best position to correct, if necessary, using suggestions from staff, students, and parents. The changes, however, will be made by the principal, superintendent, and maybe the school board, with the *principal* taking the initiative. Essentially, the 2SS requires strong principals who are not authoritarian but *know how to lead*. Authoritarian leaders would not belong in the establishment or in the functioning of the 2SS.

The leaders would discuss with those concerned the many advantages of the 2SS. In particular, the leaders would talk with teachers' unions, school support staff, parents, and the business community, as well as to the general public. The superintendent or his or her delegates would arrange meetings with other important leaders in the education community. Among them would be representatives from the local teachers' union, representation from the local school board, student council representatives, leaders from workers unions, chairpersons from home-and-school committees, the chief from the local native band, and interested local church leaders. General support from the whole community would be helpful.

When choosing a new principal, the school board would be wise to consult with the teaching staff. The salary offered for the position of principal should be high enough that the hiring team will have well-qualified, talented candidates to choose from. However, good working conditions will attract and *keep* real talent better than a high salary will. School boards should choose their principals and superintendents first, for their well-rounded education; second, for their administrative know-how; and third, for their dedication to education for *all* children. The agreement when hiring a principal must provide for termination possible at the end of one year's employment. Once the board has a good superintendent and competent principals, they can become *very* helpful in choosing new teachers.

When principals left the teachers' union in British Columbia, Canada, some years ago, their tenure depended more on ability to save money than on quality education for our children. Governments today see global trade and free enterprise as their first priority. Quality public school education is not nearly as important to them. Parents and teachers take what they are given and then do the best they can for the children in their care. But it is far from good enough.

How, then, can we save our children's future? By being and establishing community leaders who hire quality principals.

Cooperating with Each Other

Cooperation between people requires that two or more people agree on how they are going to work toward an agreed goal. This means that, to begin with, they must understand each other's reasons and methods. This alone may take some effort before cooperation is possible. It is counterproductive to demand flatly, "You had better cooperate with me." Parents who are not experienced in the skill of cooperating can, without realizing it, damage their own child's chances to do well in *any* school, no matter how good it is.

I remember when I was teaching in an elementary school of about 120 students, our very effective (and popular) principal was monitoring an intelligent student, James, in grade four because he was not doing as well as expected in math and language, although he had had very good teachers. The child was absent for two days with no explanation. The latest rumor had it that the boy's father had planned to spend some time with his friends in the next village for a week and then decided, on the spur of the moment, to take little James with him.

The principal was very angry. He was not pleased to see this child's education being messed up so early in his schooling. The school had a carefully planned program in which James had been improving noticeably. This progress was dashed when the father did not even think to ask the teacher or principal whether or not taking him out of school for a few days was a good idea.

Some parents do not consider how much planning and forethought teaching a whole class can involve and how interrupting this plan sets a child back in learning and, sometimes and more importantly, causes the child to lose interest and to feel negative about schoolwork, partly because of the interruption and partly because the pupil no longer understands what the lessons are about—a very disappointing result.

Parents and teachers need time to meet, so that they can get to know each other well enough to be able to decide how best to cooperate in the interests of the children. It does take *both* to get the good results that everybody wants. Cooperation helps continuity.

In today's overloaded classes and larger schools, teachers cannot notice each child's immediate needs. The result is that some children will lose interest in the subject. They may still do what they can, but they will no longer find the course interesting.

When solving a serious problem, the people who make decisions need to have time and energy to find out what the other involved people think and feel. From there, some joint planning can begin. For one, parents must achieve the best possible routine for their children at home and then find out how best to cooperate with what the school is trying to do for their children.

Because of government cutbacks in funding, Canadian and American school personnel are generally working under more strain in and out of the classroom. Children and teachers feel the strain, but most other adults are generally quite unaware of it. So really the best that parents can do, until we get the 2SS, is to learn to cooperate with other responsible people to improve the learning climate for their children at school and invest the time and energy to give their own children a very good start every morning at home. This would include establishing healthy habits, such as

- having no cell phones, TVs, or computers in children's bedrooms;
- ensuring early bedtimes;
- ensuring that children rise early;
- making a good breakfast available; and
- creating a well-established, smooth routine for the mornings.

Parents would need to encourage their children to respect their parents, teachers, siblings, and classmates. Although much of what I suggest here is, probably, not really possible under today's circumstances, *we must make the effort*, because giving up on helping our children get their education is unjustifiable neglect of our own kids.

Parents who are themselves not yet having problems with their children would probably be interested in building their society to match their own successful lifestyles and ensuring that their grandchildren do not lose out on the benefits. Even these successful parents are too stressed to have the energy to push for a 2SS, however desirable or necessary it may be. But without their strong demand for real improvement, the present increasing deterioration in learning conditions will continue. The government can provide better schools only if there is a strong demand for the money to finance them. In a democracy, citizens are parts of the will and the power in the country. If you expect no improvements now for your school, your children could easily be witnessing even further deterioration in opportunities for *their* children's education. Parents' interest in the future educational opportunities within their own communities makes for a strong, enduring democratic country. There is still much to be lost in the lives of successful families. If we cannot turn this destructive trend around now, today's lucky children and their families will become the big losers.

The proposed 2SS is not a panacea for education. But neither are the other new and old forms of schooling (religious schools, voucher programs, Waldorf, magnet and charter schools, Montessori, Summerhill, and other forms of private schools). The 2SS has the important advantage of being a public school and of being inclusive. The public school is well balanced in many respects and has stood the test of time in some respects.

Children with strong family support do very well in our public schools. Unfortunately, many of today's children are missing some of that kind of encouragement at home because both parents work away from home. Today's children spend much time with just each other, thereby not learning how to grow up. Children need to make their connections with the real world (as opposed to the virtual heaven of video, TV, and computer games) in order to mature mentally and emotionally as they get older.

Technology does not replace the motivation that *teachers* and *parents* used to give our children. Computers do not have feelings. They cannot nurture or recognize the child as a person. To grow in character, a child requires much interaction with a caring parent or teacher.

The 2SS would provide children with more interaction with teachers by putting them in smaller classes for a larger part of the day. Professional teachers with proper support can be most successful. We must be ready to supply these professionals with what they need and then allow them a couple of years to sort things out. In two or three years of Cool School, this new institution could be a very effective, pleasant, smooth-running school.

We can't do justice to the education of our children unless we understand that it is as important as our health care system or the environment, or at least as important as private profit taking.

As one very successful teacher and parent related to me, "The role of child care has been, for some time, and is today, the least respected job in our society, placing somewhere below you-know-who."

We cannot continue to ignore the real needs of children, who require, at present, the missing warmth and the nurturing from adults, who neglect them in favor of other duties. Children from both rich and poor families are suffering severe neglect, and it will take something other than just money to build a future for not only the economically challenged but also for the "well-to-do."

Because in the 2SS, the proper raising of children is the community's first priority, this system has a chance of being much better than the one we have now. However, because so many people are involved, there would need to be many minor adjustments as we fine-tune this cooperative support for our children's development.

The 2SS is a good plan, but its success depends on the work and commitment of parents, teachers, and other citizens. This is a human problem that requires the attention of consistent, caring adults—*not* more expensive clothes or new electronic equipment. We need to be there for the long haul.

To All Parents

Here are some helpful points for parents who want to know how to judge the quality of the present schooling that their child is receiving. This will take some of your time. So first plan accordingly with your child. Be prepared to be less critical and more ready to praise and let your child know that you value his or her opinion. Be a good listener. Let your child do most of the talking.

1. During these positive, regular times with your child, see if you can find out
    a) what he or she likes and hates about lessons;
    b) information about his or her friends that he or she considers important
    c) information that he or she considers interesting about others your child sees every day on the school bus or around school;
    d) what your child views as the best, most interesting thing about school this year;
    e) what he or she likes to wear;
    f) how many kids have cell phones and what your child thinks of them; and
    g) whether he or she has noticed any bullies and, if so, who the bullies bother the most.
2. Keep the conversations positive, by not criticizing or by not giving too much advice; either will prevent your child from telling you what you really want to know.
3. This approach to finding out how your child feels about school this year will tell you
    a) whether this arrangement is best for your child and

b)   whether the 2SS would be an improvement.

My appeal to you as parents is to never underestimate how important you are for your child. You are their best resource he or she has, and you must embrace the right and the responsibility to act in your child's best interest. My purpose for writing this book is to support all parents in their dedication to their children.

All the best for you and your child's future.

Jane Loosmore

My Recommended Reading List ...
On Bettering Our Schools

Berry, Mary Frances
The Politics of Parenthood
(1993))Penguin Books

Bibby, Reginald W.
Canada's Teens:
Today, Yesterday, and Tomorrow
(2001) Stoddart Pub.

Bohannon, Jim
America in Crisis:
Making Things Right in a Nation
Gone Wrong
(2000) Paper Chase Press

Degaetano, Gloria
Stop Teaching Our Kids To Kill:
A Call to Action Against TV, Movie,
& Video Game Violence
(1999) Crown Publishers (Random
House)

Elium, Jean and Don
Raising A Teen-Ager :
Parents and the Nurturing of a Responsible
Teen
(1999) Celestial Art

Fisher, Robert
Head Start:
How to Develop Your Child's Mind
(1999) Souvenir Press

Gallagher, Paul
Changing Course: An Agenda for the
Real Reform of Canadian Education
(1995) OISE Press Inc.

Gilligan, James
Preventing Violence
(2001) Thames & Hudson

Glasser, William
The Quality School:
Managing Students Without
Coercion
(1992) Harper Perennial

Healy, Jane M., PhD
Endangered Minds:
Why Children Don't Think and What
We Can Do About It
(1990) (Touchstone) Simon &
Schuster

Healey, Jane M., PhD
Failure To Connect:
How Computers Affect Our Children's
Minds for Better and Worse
(1998) Simon & Schuster

Henig, Jeffry R.
Rethinking School Choice:
Limits of the Market Metaphor
(1995) Princeton University

Hern, Matt
Field Day:
Getting Society Out of School
(2003) New Star Books Ltd.

Hurtig, Mel
Pay The Rent And Feed The Kids:
The Tragedy and Disgrace of
Poverty in Canada
(2000) McLelland & Stewart
Ltd.

Kilian, Crawford
School Wars:
The Assault on BC Education
(1985) New Star Books Ltd.

Kohn, Alfie PH.D.
The Schools Our Children Deserve:
Moving beyond Traditional
Classrooms and Tougher Standards
(2000) Houghton Mifflin

Laxer, James
The Undeclared War; Class Conflict
In the Age of Cyber Capitalism
(1998) Penguin Books

Mazel, Judy and Monaco, John
Slim & Fit Kids: Raising Healthy
Children in a Fast-Food World
(1999) Health Communications
Inc. Florida

Medhus, Elisa, MD
Raising Children Who Think For
Themselves:
The Essential Qualities of Self-
Directed Children
(2001) Beyond Words Publishing,
Oregon

Neill, A.S.
Summerhill
(1960) Hart Publishing Company

Nikiforuk, Andrew
If Learning is so Natural, Why am I
going to School?: A Parent's Guide
(1994) Penguin Books

Nikiforuk, Andrew
School's Out:
The Catastrophe in Public Education
and What We Can Do about It
(1993) MacFarlane, Walter, and
Ross, Toronto

Postman, Neil
The End Of Education:
Redefining the Value of School
(1994) Vintage Books (Random
House, Inc.)

Jaccobs, Jane
Dark Age Ahead
(2004) Random House of Canada
Ltd.

Saul, John Ralston
The Doubter's Companion
(1995) Viking (Penguin)

Schlechty, Phillip C.
Schools for the 21st Century:
Leadership Imperatives for
Educational Reform
(1990)Jossey-Bass Inc.

Schlosser, Eric
Fast Food Nation: The Dark Side of
the All-American Meal
(2002) Houghton Mifflin

Smith, Hedrick
Rethinking America: Rethinking
Schools for the New Global Game
(1996) Random House

Smith, Mortimer
And Madly Teach
(1950) American Book-Stratford
Press, Inc.

Sweet, Lois
*God in the Classroom: The Controversial
Issue of Religion in Canada's Schools*
(1997) McLelland & Stewart Inc.

**Tucker, Marc S. & Codding, Judy
B.**
*Standards For Our Schools:
How to Set Them, Measure Them, and
Reach Them*
(1998) Jossey-Bass

Television Broadcasts

Fareed Zakaria, GPS
CNN

Websites

The Story of Broke with Annie Leonard
http://www.storyofstuff.org/movies-all/
story-of-broke/